Anatolia

John Thomas

Nabu Public Domain Reprints:

You are holding a reproduction of an original work published before 1923 that is in the public domain in the United States of America, and possibly other countries. You may freely copy and distribute this work as no entity (individual or corporate) has a copyright on the body of the work. This book may contain prior copyright references, and library stamps (as most of these works were scanned from library copies). These have been scanned and retained as part of the historical artifact.

This book may have occasional imperfections such as missing or blurred pages, poor pictures, errant marks, etc. that were either part of the original artifact, or were introduced by the scanning process. We believe this work is culturally important, and despite the imperfections, have elected to bring it back into print as part of our continuing commitment to the preservation of printed works worldwide. We appreciate your understanding of the imperfections in the preservation process, and hope you enjoy this valuable book.

Israel, a work published by the author in London in 1850, and republished in New York in 1851—*Anatolia is original throughout.* It is an exposition of the book of Daniel from alpha to omega, with so much of the testimonies of other prophets as is necessary to its comprehension. If a person would understand the end of Daniel he must commence at the beginning of the descriptions of what he witnessed: so if an inquirer would know the truth of what is presented in the title-page of this work, he must begin at the beginning, and having read it through, give it a second reading, verifying the positions as he proceeds by reference to the texts, that his faith may stand, not in the wisdom of man, but in the power of God. The author has been careful to assert nothing unsupported by proof; as his object has not been to amuse and astonish, but to instruct. The *dénouement* of the book of Daniel is the solution of the great Eastern Question. There is no other possible solution than what he represents. Hence, to speak rationally upon the subject men must speak according to Daniel, who was a far wiser and more intelligent statesman and politician than any now living. It is because of the profound and universal ignorance of the meaning of his writings, that secular and ecclesiastical scribes and orators so vainly speculate upon the issue of the conflict they have provoked. But the governments of the nations are blind and faithless. If they were enlightened believers on God they would be unsuitable instruments for the emergencies of the times. There is a long account to be settled between God and the world, the measure of whose iniquity is well-nigh full. The crooked policy of its rulers is working out results highly favorable for the great national retribution he has decreed. His tribunal is in the Holy City; for "there will he sit to judge all the nations;" because "his fire is in Zion, and his furnace in Jerusalem." It is manifest, then, that means must be in operation to convene the forces of the nations there, that they may receive compensation in kind for their abominable desolations with which they have overspread Jehovah's land and people. This exigency of the approaching future is the scriptural reason of that prominency which is given to the "Holy Shrines in Jerusalem" in the present Eastern Question. The Holy Land and City will increase in political importance as the war proceeds; till the struggle will be not to keep Russia out of Constantinople, but to preserve Jerusalem from his dominion. The endeavor, however, will be without avail; the Czar will take the city—but after that, *"The Deluge!"*

To the household of faith, and to Israelites, this work will be found particularly interesting and important. It will demonstrate to both classes that the day of their redemption is dawning. It will enable them to discern the signs of the times, which are so luminously indicative of His appearing, whose right it is to reign. Jews by nature and adoption have suffered long and grievously at the hand of the oppressor who has scattered and peeled them by his severities. But the day of retribution approaches, when they shall "Reward Babylon even as she rewarded them, and double unto her double according to her works: in the cup that she hath filled, double shall they fill to her." Therefore, "Rejoice over her, thou heaven, and ye holy apostles and prophets: for God will then have *avenged you on her.*" These are the words of him who said, "Heaven and earth shall pass away, but my words shall not fail." This is the principle—*Vengeance on Babylon for his people's sake;* a principle overlooked by the knight-errants of the till, whose amplest conceptions extend not beyond their balance-sheets and "the light within!"

Having, then, now introduced the reader to the great subject of this work, he is invited to proceed, being well assured that when he shall have reached the end, he will admit that, the Bible being received as true, the startling propositions embodied in the title necessarily result from the establishment of the things herein proved to be noted in the scriptures of truth by his friend and well-wisher,

Mott Haven, Westchester Co., New York.

THE AUTHOR.

INDEX OF SECTIONS.

	Introductory Remarks,	3
1.	The Origin and Extent of the Kingdom of Babylon,	7
2.	The Kingdom of Men in its various Phases,	10
3.	The Lion-Phasis of the Kingdom of Babylon,	10
4.	The Bear-Phasis,	11
5.	The Four-Headed Leopard-Phasis,	11
6.	The Ten-Horned Dragon-Phasis,	13
7.	The Holy Ones of the High Ones, and their People,	16
8.	A Season and Time,	19
9.	Origin of the Romano-Greek Babylonian Sovereignty,	19
10.	The Evening-Morning Object,	23
11.	"The Holy shall be avenged,"	24
12.	Prophecy of the Seventy Weeks,	26
13.	Corrected Version of the Prophecy,	27
14.	"Messiah the Prince,"	33
15.	What should befall Judah in the Latter Days,	37
16.	Paraphrase of the Eleventh of Daniel to the thirty-fifth verse inclusive,	39
17.	End of the Maccabean Heptade,	45
18.	"The King," or Constantinopolitan Autocracy,	45
19.	A God of Guardians, or the Latin Prophet of the West,	49
20.	Guardians' Bazaars, or Temples dedicated to Saints,	53
21.	The Holy Roman Dominion, or Little Horn of the West,	56
22.	"The Time of the End,"	60
23.	The King of the North,	62
24.	Proof of the Russian Power being the King of the North,	64
25.	Future Magnitude of the Czar's Dominion,	68
26.	Nebuchadnezzar's Image the Symbol of the Autocrat's Dominion inclusive of France,	69
27.	Edom, Moab, and Ammon divided off from Turkey for a Price,	71
28.	Britain, the Moabitish Antagonist to Russia in the Latter Days,	74
29.	The Latter Days,	76
30.	The "Time of Trouble;" Position of the Russian and British Forces at the Advent,	77
31.	The Deliverance of Israel out of the Hand of their Enemies,	80
32.	Resurrection to Judgment in the War of God Almighty,	83
33.	"The Wise,"	85
34.	The Times of the Kingdom of Babylon and of Judah,	87
35.	Calendar of the Seven Times of Babylon and Judah,	99

The Old Arms of France.

Rev. xvi. 13.

ANATOLIA:

BEING AN

Exposition of Prophecy

RELATING TO

APPROACHING POLITICAL DEVELOPMENTS

AMONG THE NATIONS OF THE EARTH.

1. THE ORIGIN AND EXTENT OF THE KINGDOM OF BABYLON.

In taking a general survey of the contents of the Book of Daniel, it may be seen that *two great powers* are the principal subjects of its predictions. The one is styled "THE KINGDOM OF MEN;"[1] and the other, "THE KINGDOM OF GOD."[2]

It is true, that there are many symbols, such as the Image, the Fiery Furnace, the Tree-Stump banded with brass and iron, the Four Beasts, the Ram, and the He-Goat; but these are signs in the prophetic heraldry, not of kingdoms distinct and independent of those which have preceded them, but of one and the same *Kingdom of Men* in the several phases of its existence.

The Kingdom of Men was founded by Nimrod, son of Cush, who was son of Ham, son of Noah. "The beginning of it was Babylon, and Ereck, and Accad, and Calneh, in the land of Shinar. Out of that land he went forth into Assyria, and builded Nineveh, and the city of Rehoboth, and Calah, and Resen between Nineveh and Calah: the same is a great city."[3] This Nimroudia was the Kingdom of Men in the extent of it during the lifetime of its founder, comprehending, as we see, Babylon and Assyria. These were its roots and trunk, which in after ages came to be famous for their strength and altitude, the beauty of their leaves, the abundance of their fruits, and their wide-spreading top; so that all the nations had shadow under it, and their rulers and great men dwelt in the boughs, and all flesh were fed of it.[4]

As a magnificent "tree in the midst of the earth, whose height reached unto heaven, and the sight thereof to the end of all the earth," *the Kingdom of Men* had become under the proud-hearted Nebuchadnezzar, the destroying lion of his age.[5] He had grown and become strong; "for his greatness had grown, and reached unto heaven, and his dominion to the end of the earth."[6] In this testimony "*the end of the earth*" is defined by the extent of the dominion of the Kingdom of Men. It does not extend to the entire globe, for an immense proportion of it has

---

(1) Dan. iv. 17.   (2) Dan. ii. 44; iv. 3; vii. 27.   (3) Gen. x. 8.   (4) Dan. iv. 10—12.
(5) Jer. iv. 7; l. 17.   (6) Dan. iv. 22.

ever been beyond the limits of this kingdom. All Europe, America, and China were beyond "the end of the earth" when Nebuchadnezzar sat upon the throne of the Kingdom of Men. But, when the brazen-coated Greeks under Alexander the Macedonian established themselves in Babylon, the limits of "the earth" were enlarged; for in speaking of the "third kingdom of brass," Daniel revealed to Nebuchadnezzar, that it should "*bear rule over all the earth.*" When this was accomplished, "the end of the earth" advanced into Europe, and was defined by the western limit of Alexander's Macedonian Kingdom. But "the end of the earth" was not yet fixed even then; for when the Iron kingdom annexed the brazen dominions to a considerable extent, it removed "the end of the earth" to the Atlantic Ocean. The present constitution of the Iron Kingdom has enlarged "the earth" far beyond the shadow of the Assyrian tree when it represented the greatness of the Kingdom of Men under the Chaldean dynasty. It now comprehends "*the Holy Roman Empire,*" or Little Horn of the West, which includes papal Germany, of which Austria is the chief dominion. From the Indus, then, (the eastern limit of the Kingdom of Men under the Macedonian Dynasty,) to the German and Atlantic Oceans, comprehending Affghanistan, Persia, Media, Nimroudia, the Holy Land, Egypt, Arabia, Asia Minor, the rest of the pagan Roman dominion, the Austrian Empire, and the papal states of Germany—is the territory, styled in prophetic language "*the earth,*" upon which, since the days of Nimroud, has existed, still exists, and will continue to exist, the Kingdom of Men until it i destroyed by the Kingdom of God.

From these remarks upon "the end of the earth," it will be seen, that the Kingdom of Men has been diversified in its constitution, extent, and throne, since its foundation by Nimroud to the present time. It has nevertheless been the same Nimroudian kingdom, with Babylon and Assyria for its characteristics. Cyrus the Persian is styled King of Babylon, and Artaxerxes, King of Assyria. Though of the Persian stock, having no consanguinity with Nebuchadnezzar, they were as much kings of Assyria and Babylon as he. Alexander the Great, though a Greek, and the Seleucidæ who succeeded him in that region, were also kings of Assyria and Babylon. When the Romans got the ascendancy in the Kingdom of Men, *they banded the stump of its tree with iron and brass:*[1] and converted their own city into the "*Great Babylon*" of the dominion, which by the edict of Caracalla became coëxtensive with the dominion itself; so that Babylon, as the name of the Empire, came again to stand by the great river Euphrates, where Nimrod had originally planted the tree.

The different *forms* which the Kingdom of Men has assumed since the overthrow of Nineveh, are represented in the before-named symbols of the Book of Daniel. The metallic image is that kingdom as it will exist when Gōg comes to fall upon the mountains of Israel. If the observer take up a position contemporary with that crisis, and view the Kingdom of Men as it will then have existed from the beginning of its ascendancy over the House of Judah or of David, he will perceive that it has assumed *five* distinct forms; such as, the Chaldean, the Medo-Persian, the Macedonian or Grecian, the Roman, and the Russian; represented in the order of their enumeration by the gold, the silver, the brass, the iron, and the clay. But all the important characteristics of the Kingdom of Men in relation to the House of David and the saints (the Heirs of the divine government styled the Kingdom of God) and Judah, could not be exhibited in a compound metallic image of a man; it was, therefore, necessary to introduce other symbols for its elucidation. In the third chapter of Daniel, we are presented with an interesting illustration of the impiety and blasphemy of the Kingdom of Men; of its hostility to the people of the House of David, or the Jews, whether such by nature, or by

---

[1] Dan. iv. 15.

walking in the steps of the faith of Abraham, or by adoption; of the furnace of affliction through which they would have to pass in rejecting the superstitions of the Kingdom of Men, and in adhering to the truth of God; of their meeting with the Deliverer in their extremity; of the destruction of their tormentors; of their final deliverance; and of the ascription at last of blessing, and honor, and glory, and power to the God of Israel by the assembled nations, when God's people shall be promoted to the direction of human affairs, and the Kingdom of Men shall be no more. Nebuchadnezzar, in referring to his dream, and to the wonderful deliverance of Shadrach, Meshach, and Abednego, and to the Tree-Stump banded with Brass and Iron, styles them "*signs* and *wonders* that the High God hath wrought towards me." He might well exclaim, "How great are his *signs!* and how mighty are his *wonders!* His Kingdom is an everlasting Kingdom, and his dominion from generation to generation.

By the Image-Sign, Nebuchadnezzar learned for the first time, that the God of Israel was above all gods and kings; and that He intended, notwithstanding the Chaldæo-Babylonish conquest of Judah, and reduction of their city and temple to ruin, to have a kingdom among the generations of men, which in turn should destroy their kingdom, originally founded by Nimrod.

By the fiery-furnace "wonder" he was taught, that God would deliver his servants that trust in him with a salvation which would make them invulnerable to human power, and fit to possess the kingdom "which shall not be left to other people." And, by the sign of the Tree, and the wonder, of which he was the subject in his own person, he learned, that the rulers in the Kingdom of Men could not do as they pleased; that those who attained to high places in it (as in his own case) were such as He sets up as the most fitting instruments to work out his purposes; and that the only kingdom that will be everlasting on earth is HIS OWN, which is to grind to powder and bring to an end all the kingdoms of the Babylonish Confederacy of the Latter Days. These signs and wonders greatly enlightened the mind and subdued the pride of Nebuchadnezzar. He came to know that "*the Heavens do rule;*" or, as Paul expresses it, "The existing powers are subjected to God"—ὑπο του Θεου; an elliptical expression for *under the Angels of God.**

The fifth chapter informs us how the Chaldean Royalty was finished, and the Kingdom of Men transferred to the Medes and Persians; whose dynasty is represented in the seventh and eighth chapters by a Bear with three Ribs between its teeth, and by a Ram with horns of unequal height. The Medo-Persian Royalty of the Kingdom of Men is represented in the Image by the Breast and the Arms of Silver; and as the Image is to exist complete in the Latter Days, Persia must be a constituent of the dominion represented by it. Persia will, therefore, be certainly confederate with Russia at the overthrow of the Autocrat.

But, an interesting announcement was made to Belshatzar, styled by Isaiah "Lucifer, son of the morning," before he fell from heaven to go down to the sides of the pit.[1] It was, that *his kingdom was numbered*, and, as far as his family was concerned, "finished." It was relatively finished, not absolutely so; because this finished kingdom was to "be divided, and given to the Medes and Persians." The kingdom was numbered, and his tenure of it likewise. His occupation of the throne as a member of the golden dynasty had been limited to the seventieth year from the first of Nebuchadnezzar's reign.[2] These seventy years were filled up by Nebuchadnezzar's reign of forty-four years; Evil-Merodach's, of two years; Usurp-

---

* Paul says, that "God has not put in subjection the *future* habitable to the angels;" which is tantamount to saying, that the present habitable, or territory of the Kingdom of Men, is put under the angels. The same territory in the future will be subjected to Jesus and his brethren. Heb. ii. 5, 8–10.

(1) Isai. xiv. 4, 12, 15.   (2) Jer. xxvii. 7; xxv. 12.

ers', of four years and nine months; and Belshatzar's, grandson of Nebuchadnezzar, of nineteen years and three months. The Scripture takes no notice of the usurpers; I have therefore divided the twenty-six years remaining after the death of Nebuchadnezzar in the thirty-seventh of Jehoiachin's captivity, between Evil-Merodach and Belshatzar in my chronology at the end of Elpis Israel. But the Kingdom of Men, which passed from the golden into the silver constitution of the empire, had been numbered, as well as the duration of its Chaldean dynasty. Nebuchadnezzar was not only informed that the Kingdom of Men should fight its last battle with the Kingdom of God "*in the latter days*," but a sign and a wonder were given him by which he might know *how far remote from his times* those appointed days should be. The decree of the Watchers concerning the duration of the kingdom, or Banded Stump, is, "*Let seven times pass over him.*" When these *seven times* should approach their termination the latter days of the Kingdom of Men would have arrived; and with them the time for the final overthrow of it by "THE STONE cut out of the mountain which was not in hands." But of these *seven times* I shall write more particularly hereafter.

2. THE KINGDOM OF MEN IN ITS VARIOUS PHASES.

In the first year of Belshatzar's reign, which was nineteen before his overthrow by Cyrus, further particulars were represented concerning the relation of the Kingdom of Men, or Serpent-power, to Messiah the Prince and his coadjutors, through whom at length the might of God's Kingdom was to be brought to bear on the Serpent-kingdom for its utter destruction at the end of the Seven Times. These things were not represented to the King of Babylon, but to Daniel himself, as specially interested in them.

In the vision of the Four Beasts he saw the Kingdom of Babylon in its golden, silver, brazen, iron, and iron and clay manifestations. Through these distinct symbols he saw what could not be represented in a statue, where the metals in juxtaposition signified merely *one united dominion in the latter days*. By the Four Beasts he saw that the successive phases through which the Kingdom of the Serpent was to pass, were to result from the tempest of war in the Mediterranean countries. His words are, "The four winds of the heaven strove upon the Great Sea, and four great beasts came up from the sea, diverse from one another." The winds were not all blowing at once, but successively and at long intervals, each tempest resulting in a change in the constitution and government of the Kingdom of Babylon, as represented by the Beasts. By these belligerent tempests the Macedonian-brass and the Roman-iron dynasties, incorporated themselves with the gold and silver Babylonish dominion, and with one another forming thus the Band of Iron and Brass, and setting itself around the Tree-Stump when the royalty should be transferred to Rome as the seat or throne of the power in its fourth beast or dragon manifestation.

3. THE LION-PHASIS OF THE KINGDOM OF BABYLON.

The Beasts being substituted for the metals of Nebuchadnezzar's Image, they represent of course the same phases of the Kingdom of Men. We learn from Jeremiah that the powers of Nineveh and Babylon were each represented by *lions*. He says, "Israel is a scattered sheep; the *lions* have driven them away: first the King of Assyria hath devoured him; and last this Nebuchadnezzar King of Babylon hath broken his bones."[1] The Ninevite Assyrian was represented to Daniel as *a lion with eagle's wings*. Many years before, God had punished the King of Assyria and his land for scattering the Ten Tribes by transferring the dominion over the Nimroudian empire from Nineveh to Babylon. This revolution is represented by

---

(1) Jer. 1. 17.

the eagle-wings being "*plucked*" from the lion's back; while the lion itself was made to stand erect as a man, and to receive in exchange for its lion-heart, the heart of a man. Thus the Lion-Man became the symbol of the Kingdom of Babylon so long as the government continued in the family of Nebuchadnezzar; which with all its faults was more human than that which it succeeded.

4. THE BEAR-PHASIS.

The impiety of Belshazzar brought ruin upon his family and calamity upon the Kingdom. It was made an accusation against him by Daniel that "the God in whose power his breath was, and whose were all his ways, he had not glorified." Convicted of this, the Lord of heaven pronounced sentence upon him, saying, "God hath numbered thy reign, and finished it. Thou art weighed in the balances and found wanting. Thy Kingdom is divided, and given to the Medes and Persians." The execution of this sentence was prompt; for "on that night was Belshatzar the King of the Chaldeans slain. And Darius the Median took the Kingdom."

This transfer of the government occurred B. C. 538. Its mission was to restore Judah's Commonwealth, and to extend the boundary of the Kingdom of Men. "*Arise, devour much flesh,*" was the policy of its reign. The Bear was the symbol of this government, whose dominion extended from India to Ethiopia, over a hundred and twenty-seven provinces. The reign of the Bear began under a Mede, and in two years passed by inheritance to Cyrus, a Persian. This change of position was represented to Daniel in the saying that "*it raised up itself on one side,*" so that one side became "higher than the other;" but before it raised itself up, the higher side was no higher than the other; therefore the higher side acquired its position last, as appears in the history of the time. The Ram in the eighth chapter with horns of unequal height is another symbol for the same government: the unequal elevation of the sides of the Bear, and the different altitude of the Ram's horns, are conditions representative of the same dynastic peculiarity—"*The higher horn came up last.*"

The Bear had also another peculiarity worthy of note. "It had three ribs in the mouth of it between its teeth." These ribs represented the threefold division of its conquests. The interpretation is found elsewhere in these words of Daniel: "it pleased Darius to set over the Kingdom a hundred and twenty princes, who should be over the whole Kingdom; and over these, *three Presidents*, of whom Daniel was chief: that the princes might give account to them, and the King (the Bear-Mouth) should have no damage." The three presidencies, then, of the silver dominion were the ribs in the mouth of the Bear.

In dismissing this symbol, it is worthy of remark, that while the *Ram*, by which the Persians represented themselves in Daniel's time, is their symbol in relation to the Macedonians under Alexander, God has chosen for them the *Bear* to signify them as an element of the Image in the latter-days. The latter-day symbol then of Persia, is a Bear; and a Bear is at this time her formidable neighbor, and has already taken from her a large portion of her territory. The Russian Bear is destined to supersede her present government as an independent sovereignty, and to grasp Persia between its teeth from near India to Ethiopia, which is to be "*at his steps.*" This is no mere conjecture, but absolutely certain; for Jehovah has declared by Ezekiel that Persia shall be an element of Gog's confederacy, and that Gog's is the Russian power will be seen when I come to treat of the King of the North at the time of the end. The Ram continued 206 years and 9 months.

5. THE FOUR-HEADED LEOPARD-PHASIS.

The third symbol representative of the Kingdom of Babylon under a new constitution shown to Daniel, was a Leopard with Four Heads and Four Wings. It answers to the brazen part of the Image, which "bore rule over all the earth;" and to the Goat with Four Horns pointing to the Four Winds in the eighth chapter; but *without the Little Horn, which is represented by the fourth Beast.* The Leopard is Macedonian, representing Alexander the Great's dominion and those of his four principal successors who divided it among themselves. The body of the beast represents the power before it was divided; and each head one of the subsequent divisions. The wings represented the position of the Macedonian Heads relatively to the Holy Land. At the death of Alexander a long period of war ensued, which resulted B. C. 301 in the establishment of the following Kingdoms on the territory of the Kingdom of Men.

First Head.—The Kingdom of the South, comprehending Egypt, Libya, Arabia, Cœle-Syria, and Palestine, under the Ptolemies.

Second Head.—The Kingdom of the north-west, including Thrace, Bythinia, etc., or the Thraco-Macedonian.

Third Head.—The Kingdom of the north-east, comprehending the rest of Asia inclusive of Babylon and its province; and extending beyond the Euphrates to the Indus. India beyond that river, though allotted to this head, revolted; so that the Indus became its boundary. This was the *Macedo-Babylonish* Kingdom of the Seleucidæ.

Fourth Head.—The Kingdom of the West, embracing Macedonia and Greece.

The Lion-Man, the Bear, the Leopard, and its Third Head, or Kingdom of the North, all established themselves in the city of Babylon, where Alexander "held, as it were, the States-General of the world," and which he had resolved to make the throne of his empire. But the decree of heaven was against the city.[1] The purpose of Alexander was frustrated by death; and by B. C. 293, it became an uninhabited desert by the inundation of the Euphrates and the building of Seleucia on the banks of the Tigris about forty miles above, to which its citizens removed. Thus, the tree of Babylon was hewn down, its branches lopped, its leaves shaken off, and its fruit scattered; so that the nations got away from under it, and their rulers from its branches. Nevertheless, the Stump of its roots remained[2] under the sovereignty of the Third Head of the Leopard, founded by Seleucus, for almost 250 years; when the iron and brass became one dominion in Asia by the annexation of the Macedo-Babylonish territory to the Roman; and the band being thus formed, it was found at length encircled by it B. C. 65.

Of the four heads of the Leopard and the four horns of the Goat, but *two only* figure in the prophecy of Daniel's book. The reason of this is, that the prophecy was not delivered to prefigure the history of the Gentiles; but *to foreshow how the international policy of some of them in its bearing upon Judah, the Holy Land, and the saints, would at length create such a situation of affairs in the end, as would favor the execution of the divine purpose of demolishing the powers of the Gentiles in the establishing of the Kingdom of God.* "The secret of the Lord is with them that fear him." The matter is therefore revealed for the information of those that obey him, that they may not be taken unawares. "The wise shall understand." Let them know, then, that the policy of only two heads of the Leopard is foreshown, because they only of the four had to do with Judah and the Holy Land; and were sufficient to connect the iron with the silver of the Image. Hence, the undivided dominion of Alexander was the Belly, and these two heads also the two Thighs of brass; and therefore continuous with the iron Roman-Leg: so that the brass and iron limbs of the Image from hip to ankle represent the fourth form in its Greco-Roman constitution. The two thighs and the two heads represent the Kingdom of the South, and the Kingdom of the North-east, as above defined; and with the Little Horn of the Goat, or eastern element of the Fourth Beast, in relation to Judah

---

(1) Isai. xiv. 22, 23; xiii. 19, 22.　　　　(2) Dan. iv. 14, 15.

and the Holy Land, are the powers of the eleventh chapter from the fifth verse to the end.

6. THE TEN-HORNED DRAGON-PHASIS OF THE KINGDOM OF BABYLON.

The previous beasts were introduced into this prophecy as the basis of the fourth, which in many points was diverse from them all. Daniel says, "it was dreadful and terrible, and strong exceedingly, and *it had great iron teeth*." The *iron* teeth connect it with the iron legs, and iron element of the iron-clay Feet and Toes. *Its claws were of brass;* which shows that it is related also to the power represented by the brazen parts of the Image. These two metals being inserted in the symbol suggest the power it was designed to represent—a dominion constituted of the Greek and Latin elements. Has such a dynastic form of the Kingdom of Babylon ever existed? The history of the nations of the Mediterranean countries from B. C. 65 to A. D. 395, shows that such a dynastic manifestation not only existed, but "*devoured and brake in pieces*," as predicted it would; though *it has not yet* "*stamped the residue with its brazen-clawed Feet*." The power existing during this period chose to represent itself by a *Dragon;* we may, therefore, as Daniel has given it no name, style it for convenience THE GRECO-ROMAN DRAGON.

It had Ten Horns. They stood up as long as the beast continued in life; but not all: for three of them fell before an eleventh that came up on the beast afterwards. Seven strong horns and three broken, or "plucked up by the roots." These ten horns thus conditioned, with the brazen-clawed feet, represent the same things as the iron-clay feet and toes of the Image. When the Russo-Greek elements (clay and brass) are combined with the Gomerians (iron) in the Gog confederacy, the feet of the Greco-Roman Dragon will be manifested; and it will then "stamp the residue with the feet of it." Hitherto the Dragon has destroyed with its "*great iron teeth;*" hereafter it will use its feet and claws. The Feet of the Image, and the Feet of the Dragon, have yet to be formed out of existing elements; and it is the King of the North's mission to accomplish the work.

The Horns of the Dragon, and the Toes of the Image, represent kingly powers, or thrones; which are to exist until the taking possession of the Dragon-dominion by the Saints shall be perfected. They are emblems of kingdoms existing when the judgment sits for the destruction of the kingdom of Babylon. I know of no place where it is written that the Horns and Toes were to have an uninterupted existence of 1260 years; but I do find that "The Ten Horns receive power as kings *one hour* with the beast"[1]—that is, *thirty years;* so that we need not be careful to identify them until then.

After the Horns had struck their roots into the Dragon territory, an eleventh "came up among them" which Daniel characterizes as "*a Little Horn.*" In order to make room for itself it subdued three of the ten, and incorporated their territories into its own dominion. This incorporation made it imperial—*an Emperorship in the midst of Seven Kingdoms;* so that it stood as the Eighth Power.

But this eighth power was diverse from the Seven; in that it had the *Eyes of a Man* which gave it a more audacious look than the others; and a *mouth* by which it spake very great words on behalf of (לצד *l'tzad,* for the side of) the High ones, ... thinking to change times and laws. The eyes and mouth of the Little Horn were sufficient for all the rest. Its undertaking to speak as the representative of the High Ones in regard to times and laws connects the mouth with matters spiritual, showing that the horn, eyes, and mouth, are emblematical of a civil, military, and ecclesiastical power. This power manifested itself originally in Rome A. D. 800, as the Western Roman, or "HOLY ROMAN EMPIRE;" of which I shall speak more particularly hereafter. Suffice it to say here, that while the jurisdiction of

---

[1] Rev. xiii. 12.

the secular element of the horn has been limited to its proper territory; the spiritual dominion of the Eyes and Mouth has reigned in the kingdoms of all the horns of the Dragon-territory ceded to the western beast.

In the countries ruled by these eight horns have existed classes of people against which, under the influence of the Eyes and Mouth, they have entertained unmitigated and cruel hatred. They have poured out their blood like water, and harassed them with all possible pains and penalties. The *enmity* that has obtained between these Horn-powers and these classes has been mutual and implacable; so that war between them could only be finally extinguished by the conquest of one party or the other. These classes are called קַדִּישִׁין, *kaddishin*, that is, *Holy Ones*; whose fate has been to be overcome by *the imperial and regal papal powers of Babylon*. This was foreshown to Daniel in these words, "*I beheld, and the same Little Horn made war with the holy ones, and prevailed against them.*" The subjugation of the holy ones, however, was not a finality. God never intended that the Seed of the Woman should be bruised in the head, or finally crushed; this is a fate in reserve for the Serpent-power and its adherents. All that this can do against "the holy ones of the Most High" is to bruise them in the heel, which is as curable, and in the same way, as the wound it inflicted on Jesus, when on the accursed tree (styled by the Seed of the Serpent "*Holy Cross*") "the iniquity of his heels compassed him about"—that is, *by a resurrection from among the dead to eternal life at the coming of Messiah*. It is therefore only until the time of this event that the Imperio Regal Papacy of the Babylonish dominion prevails over the Holy Ones of the Most High; as it is written, "*The Little Horn prevailed against them*, UNTIL *the Ancient of Days came*." Here is a point of time beyond which the misfortunes of the Holy Ones do not extend. It is the turning-point in their career in relation to the "dreadful and terrible, and exceedingly strong" dominion that makes such dreadful havoc on the earth—a dominion which no earth-born power can subdue.

The coming of the Ancient of Days is a great event in this prophecy. He is said to sit, and one like the Son of Man to be brought to him, after which he is said to come. When the prophecy was delivered the Son of Man had not been born; hence that peculiar representative mode of expressing: but he has since been born, and gone into a far country, where he has appeared in the presence of the Ancient of Days, or the Father, for the purpose of receiving from him "*Dominion, and glory, and a kingdom, that all people, and nations, and languages, should serve him; and all rulers obey him.*"[1] Though these things are promised to him, and though he is the heir of them all, he has not received them; as is manifest from the fact that the "all people, and nations, and languages" serve the rulers of the Gentiles, and especially that system of governments represented by the Greco-Roman Dragon. But when the time appointed arrives, as the Ancient of Days embodied in the holy spiritual nature, he will come, having received power and authority to take the dominion, glory, and kingdom, promised him. Thus the Ancient of Days comes, and "sits in Jerusalem, the Holy City, to judge all the nations round about"[2]—there he sits, "his throne being like the fiery flame, and his wheels as burning fire;" and sends forth from before him a stream of fire.

For the signification of *the Wheels* and *Fire* read Ezekiel's first and tenth chapters. They are parts of his imagery put for the whole in this text of Daniel. "The Spirit of the Living Creatures is in the Wheels." They represent the same as the four living creatures in Rev. v. 8—10. They are the "redeemed out of every kindred, and tongue, and people, and nation," raised from the dead, in consuming and destructive motion against the body and horns of the Greco-Roman Dragon. They are the thousand thousands who minister to the commands of the Ancient of Days; and go forth with him as a fiery stream against the " Beast and

---

(1) Dan. vii. 13, 14, 27; Luke xix. 12, 15.   (2) Joel iii. 12, 16.

the False Prophet, and the Kings of the earth and their armies," to give them "of the wrath of God poured out without mixture into the cup of his indignation"—thus tormenting all the adherents of the Beast and his Image with fire and brimstone in the presence of the holy messengers, and in the presence of the Lamb.[1]

When the Ancient of Days comes, this *judgment is set, and the books are opened*; and whosoever is found written in the Lamb's Book of Life awakes to everlasting life, and to a participation in the judgment upon the Four Beasts; and whosoever is not found written there is cast into the burning flame that destroys the body of the Dragon.[2]

The taking away of the dominion of Babylon, and the bringing of its kingdom to an end, is the work assigned to the Holy Ones; who in overthrowing the Gentile powers will also appropriate to their own use all they possess. Hence, at the coming of the Ancient of Days, it is testified, that the hitherto vanquished holy ones should become conquerors in their turn—should conquer the gold, and the silver, and the brass, and the iron, and the clay; or the four kingdoms of Powers that exist on the Babylonish earth, and take them for themselves: as it is written, "These great beasts which are four represent four kings, or royalties, which shall arise out of the earth. But the holy ones of the High Ones shall take the kingdom (of Babylon) and possess the kingdom for the age, even for the age of everlasting." Again, "The Ancient of Days came, and judgment was given to the holy ones of the High Ones;" when "the time came that the holy ones should possess the kingdom." And again, "Let the saints be joyful in glory; let them sing aloud upon their beds. Let the high praises of God be in their mouth, and a two-edged sword in their hand; to execute vengeance upon the nations, and punishments upon the people; to bind their kings with chains, and their nobles with fetters of iron; *to execute upon them the judgment written*: this honor have *all* his saints.[3] The "judgment written" is the judgment that sits when the Ancient of Days comes. They are not only to slay the Fourth Beast, and to destroy its body with fire and brimstone; but they are to take away the dominion of the Lion-Man, the Bear, and the Leopard; whose peoples, and nations, and languages, however, will experience a better fate than those of the Fourth Beast dominion: for, while the Latins are almost exterminated, the populations of Assyria, Persia, and Macedonian Egypt, are permitted to retain their nationality *for a season and time*. That they do remain distinct national organizations is evident from the following testimonies: "In that day shall there be a highway out of Egypt to Assyria, and the Assyrian shall come into Egypt, and the Egyptian into Assyria, and the Egyptians shall serve with the Assyrians. In that day shall Israel be the third with Egypt and with Assyria, a blessing in the midst of the land; whom Jehovah of armies shall bless, saying, Blessed be Egypt my people, and Assyria the work of my hand, and Israel mine inheritance."[4] And, "I will set my throne in Elam, and will destroy from thence the king of princes: but it shall come to pass *in the latter days*, I will bring again the captivity of Elam, saith Jehovah."[5]

The manner in which the dominion of Assyria and Elam or Persia is taken away when the judgment sits is revealed in Micah's prophecy concerning him who was to be born in Bethlehem "*to be Ruler in Israel*," that is, concerning Jesus who was born there. He writes, "And He shall stand and rule in the strength of Jehovah, in the majesty of the name of Jehovah his God; and they (Israel) shall abide; for now shall he (Jesus) be great unto the ends of the earth. And this (Jesus) shall be the peace of (Israel) when the Assyrian (the king of the north or Gog) shall come into our land: and when he shall tread in our fortresses, then shall we raise against him seven leaders, even eight anointed ones of Adam—אָדָם, *adam*. And

---

(1) Rev. xiv. 10; xix. 19–21. (2) Rev. xx. 15; xxi. 27.
(3) Ps. cxlix. 5-9.   (4) Isai. xix. 23.   (5) Jer. xlix. 38.

they shall waste the land of Assyria with the sword, and the land of Nimrod in the entrances thereof: thus shall he (Jesus) deliver from the Assyrian, when he cometh into our land, and when he treadeth within our borders."[1] These eight anointed ones are some of the holy ones with the Ancient of Days who execute judgment at his appearing.

But, at what time does he appear? This is found by attending to what is said concerning the Little Horn power and the holy ones. It is to prevail against them until the Ancient of Days come, which "*until*" is indicated in the words, "The holy ones shall be given into his power *until* a time, and times, and the dividing of a time." Hence, the Ancient of Days will come at the end of this period, which has not yet expired; for if it had, the Ancient of Days would now be in the Holy Land, the holy ones would now be executing judgment, and the season and time would be current. There are no data in the seventh of Daniel for the calculation of the three times and a half, or 1260 years, as they are well understood to signify. All that can be known from it is, that they pertain to the Greco-Roman Dragon, that they end with the commencement of judgment upon its Little Horn, and with the beginning of the "season and time:" we must look to other testimonies to ascertain the duration of this, and the probable termination of the 1260 years.

Daniel does not tell us here how long a time after the ending of the 1260 years will be occupied in the executing of judgment by the holy ones upon the Body, Little Horn, and Ten Horns, of the fourth beast, which are to be utterly destroyed. This can be learned from another source. He contents himself for the time with informing us of the general result of the judgment in the entire and complete overthrow of the Kingdom of Babylon represented by the four beasts; and in the setting up of the kingdom by the God of heaven[2] through the agency of the holy ones inclusive of Jesus, who is their chief. Hence, he concludes the account of his vision by saying, "And the kingdom and dominion, and the greatness of the kingdom under the whole heaven shall be given to the people of the holy ones of the High Ones, whose kingdom is an everlasting kingdom, and whom all dominions shall serve and obey." This accomplished, and the kingdom will be "*restored again to Israel*,"[3] and be in the hands of those for whom it has been preparing "*from the foundation of the world*,"[4] and who once seized of it will "*not leave it to other people*," but retain it "*for ever*."

7. THE HOLY ONES OF THE HIGH ONES, AND THEIR PEOPLE.

In the seventh of Daniel there are three parties associated together in executing judgment upon the Beasts—the holy ones, the High Ones, and "the people of the holy ones." The holy ones are styled "*the saints*" in the common version; and the High Ones are termed "*the Most High*" in the singular. The word *saint* signifies *a holy one;* but it has been so misapplied by the Gentiles that I have preferred the latter, as keeping before the mind the saying, that "without holiness no man shall see Jehovah." The phrase "the Most High" in the singular number is in the plural in the Chaldee original. The word there is עֶלְיוֹנִין, *elyōnin*. This is not accidental, for it occurs four times in the same chapter, which supplies the reason of the expression, in the introduction of the Ancient of Days and the Son of Man into the vision. These are the High Ones to whom the holy ones belong; as it is written, "Ye are Christ's, and Christ is God's."

The holy ones of the High Ones take the kingdom which is then given to *the people* of the holy ones. These are the Twelve Tribes of Israel, who, *under the government of the holy ones*, possess "the kingdom and dominion, and the greatness

---

(1) Mic. v. 2–6. (2) Dan. ii. 44. (3) Acts i. 6. (4) Matt. xxv. 34.

of the kingdom under the whole heaven." They possess these in the sense in which a nation is said to possess such things, while at the same time it is only the princes and rulers of the nation who possess the glory, honor, majesty, and high offices of the kingdom. The holy ones and their Most Holy Prince will possess these with immortality, which pertains to them exclusively; while the Israelites who constitute "the people," or *subjects of the kingdom*, will stand related to the holy ones as the subjects of all other nations do to the nobility and government of their kingdoms; but with this exception that, whereas the subjects and rulers of kingdoms hitherto existing in the world have been all mortal, and therefore under the necessity of leaving their houses, dignities, and power to other people, or successors, the princes of God's kingdom in the Holy Land will be deathless, but the subjects thereof mortal.

The possessing of the kingdom and dominion and their greatness under the whole heaven of the four beasts by Israel, is predicted by the prophet Micah in these words:—"I will surely assemble all of thee, O Jacob; I will surely gather *the remnant* of Israel. . . In that day, saith Jehovah, will I assemble her that halteth, and I will gather her that is driven out, and her that I have afflicted; and I will make her that halted a remnant, and her that was cast far off a strong nation: *and the Lord shall reign over them in Mount Zion from henceforth, even for ever.* And thou, O Citadel of the flock, the stronghold of the daughter of Zion, unto thee shall it come even the First Dominion; the Kingdom shall come to the daughter of Jerusalem."¹ And by Zephaniah, Jehovah saith, "Sing, O daughter of Zion; shout, O Israel; be glad and rejoice with all the heart, O daughter of Jerusalem. The Lord hath taken away thy judgments, *he hath cast out their enemy* (the Turk and afterwards the Russian) the King of Israel, the Lord (Jesus) is in the midst of thee; *thou shalt not see evil any more.* . . . Behold, at that time I will undo all that afflict thee: and I will save her that halteth, and gather her that was driven out, and I will get them praise and fame in every land where they have been put to shame."² And again, he says by Zechariah, "Sing and rejoice, O daughter of Zion; for, lo, I (Jesus) come, and I will dwell in the midst of thee; and *many nations shall be joined to the Lord in that day, and shall be my people;* and I will dwell in the midst of thee; and the Lord shall possess Judah his portion in the Holy Land, and shall choose Jerusalem again."³ . . . "I will dwell in the midst of Jerusalem; and Jerusalem shall be called a city of truth, and the mountain of Jehovah of armies the holy mountain. "There shall yet old men and old women dwell in the streets of Jerusalem, and every man with his staff in his hand for very age. And the streets of the city shall be full of boys and girls playing in the streets thereof. For I will save my people from the east country, and from the west country; and I will bring them, and they shall dwell in the midst of Jerusalem: and they shall be my people, and I will be their God, in truth and righteousness. . . Yea, many people, and strong nations shall come to seek Jehovah of armies in Jerusalem, and to pray before the Lord. In those days ten men shall take hold out of all languages of the nations, even shall take hold of the skirt of him that is a Jew, saying, We will go with you: for we have heard that God is with you."⁴ "Then shall the children of Judah and the children of Israel be gathered together, and appoint themselves One Head, (or king,) and they shall come up out of the land (of the enemy,) for great shall be the day of Jezreel."⁵ "And I will make them one nation in the land upon the mountains of Israel; and one king shall be king to them all: and they shall be no more two nations, neither shall they be divided into two kingdoms any more at all. And THE BELOVED my servant shall be king over them: and they shall have one Shepherd: they shall also walk

---

(1) Mic. ii. 12; iv. 6. (2) Zeph. iii. 14–20. (3) Zech. ii. 10–12. (4) Zech. viii. 3–8, 22, 23. (5) Hos. i. ii.

in my judgment, and observe my statutes, and do them. And they shall dwell in the land that I have given unto Jacob my servant, wherein your fathers have dwelt; and they shall dwell therein, they, and their children, and their children's children for ever. And my servant the Beloved shall be their prince for ever."[1]

From these testimonies it is evident, that a kingdom consisting of the twelve United Tribes of Israel is to be established in the Holy Land under a king high in the favor of the Ancient of Days; and that when it exists it will have the ascendancy in the world, and be celebrated for the fame and glory of its people among all nations. It is clear also that the accomplishment of these predictions will settle all controversies about "the Holy Places," and be a quietus to all "Eastern Questions." The reduction of God's promises to accomplished facts must be the extinction, not only of the Ottoman, but of all the governments and powers of Europe and Asia; and the substitution of the Israelitish Dominion in their place, when Israel shall be Jehovah's first-born [2] among the nations of the coming age. Being the body of this kingdom, whose founders are the High Ones, and its rulers and princes their holy ones, the people of the holy ones are the constituents, or commonalty, of the body, even the twelve tribes of Israel, the nation of Jehovah.

The Holy Ones that slay the Greco-Roman Dragon, destroy its body in the burning flame of their power, and take away the dominion of the Lion-Man, Bear, and Leopard, are persons who have attained to immortality as a part of the reward promised in the gospel of the kingdom to all "who walk *in the steps* of the faith of Abraham," whose faith was made perfect by his works.[3] That they are immortals is evident, from it being affirmed of them that they possess the kingdom for ever, which those only can do who are deathless. These immortals are called holy ones, because they attain to immortality on account of their previous holiness, "without which no one can see the Lord;" that is, the High Ones of the vision. From this a very interesting question arises, namely, What did their holiness consist in that gave them acceptance with the High Ones? This is a question answered in the following words by the Spirit of God—"*The saints are they who keep the commandments of God, and the faith of Jesus.*"[4] Hence, it is written, "Blessed are they that do his commandments, that they may have right to the tree of life, and may enter in through the gates into the city;" that is, that they may have right to immortality, and may enter into the kingdom by resurrection to everlasting life.[5] The faith of Jesus is explained as being "*the testimony of Jesus*"— ἡ μαρτυρια, *hē martyria*—what is taught of Jesus Christ;[6] and "the testimony of Jesus is the spirit, or import, of the prophecy." "The words I speak unto you," said he, "they are spirit, and they are life;"[7] that is, the words I speak believed make alive. The doctrine taught by Jesus intelligently and heartily believed is spirit, from which as the germ of a new existence, holiness unto eternal life originates. The words spoken by Jesus are styled "the good message concerning the kingdom of God," το ευαγγελιον της βασιλειας, *tŏ evangelion tēs basileias*,[8] and "the words of eternal life." To those who received these words he said, "Ye are clean through the word which I have spoken to you;" and on such, purified in mind and disposition by belief of that word, he commanded his apostles to enjoin "immersion into the name of the Father, and of the Son, and of the Holy Spirit,"[9] that they might thus become the children of the High Ones.[10] Being thus by faith and obedience introduced into Christ, he is to them "wisdom, and *righteousness*, and *sanctification*, and redemption;"[11] that is, they are in a state of purity, and holy, being in him.

Having been thus constituted righteous and holy persons by being washed, sanctified, and justified in the name of the Lord Jesus, and by the Spirit of their

---

(1) Ezek. xxxvii. 22–25. (2) Exod. iv. 22. (3) Rom. iv. 12; James ii. 22. (4) Rev. xiv. 12. (5) Rev. xxii. 14. (6) Rev. xi² ¹⁷: xix. 10. (7) John vi. 63. (8) Matt. iv. 23. (9) Matt. xxviii. 19. (10) Gal. iii. 26, 27. (11) 1 Cor. i. 30.

God,[1] they thenceforth "yield their members servants to righteousness unto holiness;" for "having been made free from sin, and become servants to God, they have their fruit into holiness, and *the end* everlasting life."[2] In the vision under consideration, Daniel saw them as having attained to that end; and saw them likewise as the military chieftains of their people Israel, taking violent possession of "the kingdom and glory to which they had been called;" for "the kingdom of the heavens suffereth violence, and the violent take it by force."

8. A SEASON AND TIME.

As I have said, there is nothing in the seventh of Daniel from which can be ascertained the length of time during which Assyria, Persia, and Egypt—the southern head of the Leopard—shall continue distinct nationalities after the taking away of their dominions by the holy ones. The sentence concerning them is, that "a prolonging in life shall be given them *for a season and time.*" Now we learn from the Scriptures that there is a time when national distinctions among mankind shall have an end; *a season and time* cannot therefore be interminable. The reign of the holy ones is to be for an age, even to the age of everlasting. This age is of coëqual duration with the season and time, and conterminous with it in the age of everlasting. In the season-and-time age, then, Assyria, Persia, and Egypt, are dominionless, while the holy ones are kings in the whole heaven of the kingdom of men. But when the season and time end at the period of the opening of the age of everlasting, what then? Paul informs us, that at the end the Son of Man shall deliver up the kingdom to the Father, or Ancient of Days, having by that time put down all rule, and all authority, and power: for he must reign *till* he has put all enemies under his feet. And when all things shall be subdued unto him, then shall the Son also himself be subject to the Ancient of Days who puts all things under him, that God may be the all things in all.[3] It is evident, then, from this, that the kingdom and dominion are not to continue unchanged interminably; but that when the time comes to abolish death from the earth, that abolition will necessitate a change in the constitution of the world. The reign of the Son of Man and his holy companions *over nations of mortal men* is therefore limited by that necessity. If, then, we can find a revelation of how long they are to reign, we shall have ascertained the duration of the *season and time.* This matter was revealed to John in Patmos. He tells us that he saw one descend from heaven and bind the Dragon, so that that power could not injuriously affect the nations for 1,000 years; and that coëvally with that period he saw persons occupying thrones who reigned with Christ as the priests of God.[4]

A season and time, then, is a 1,000 years, or two times of 360 years each; and *a set time* of 280 years; or 9 months and 10 days of years, 280 days being a set time, or period of gestation.[5] For this season and time of 1,000 years the holy ones possess the world as theirs. At the end of that time, sin being eradicated, death is abolished, and their priesthood necessarily ceases. They therefore reign no more *as priests;* but God is all things in all the dwellers upon the earth.

9. ORIGIN OF THE ROMANO-GREEK BABYLONIAN SOVEREIGNTY.

In the third year of the reign of Belshatzar king of Babylon, another vision was presented to Daniel, which he has recorded in the eighth chapter of his book. It was communicated for the purpose of exhibiting certain important events in the future history of Judah, characterized by the suppression of their religious polity, the destruction of their commonwealth, and subversion of their power for a long

---

(1) 1 Cor. vi. 9–11.   (2) Rom. vi. 19–22.   (3) 1 Cor. xv. 24.   (4) Rev. xx. 1–6.
(5) Gen. xxi. 2.

series of ages; but with the consolatory assurance that God would avenge them, and by a Great Deliverer destroy the power that had so long oppressed them.

By studying the symbols of this chapter the power will be found to originate in Babylon, and to be the same as that represented by the four beasts, but without the introduction of the Ten Horns and the Little Horn with its Eyes and Mouth. These signify the Latin or papal governments of the west in their relation to the holy ones; while the Bear and the Ram, the Leopard and the He Goat, the fourth Beast, and the Little Horn of the Goat, are the heraldry of the same dynastic manifestations of the kingdom of Babylon in relation to the עַם־קְדֹשִׁים ăm-kĕdō-shim, or *people of the holy ones;* that is, THE SAINTS' NATION, in its occupancy of the Holy Land.

Daniel saw the vision while residing in Persia at the palace of Shushan, under the government of the Lion-Man, which had but sixteen years to continue over the affairs of the kingdom of Babylon. Hence, the Chaldean sovereignty being about to pass away, and sufficient having been revealed in former visions and signs, it was unnecessary to introduce it again: therefore, in the one before us the symbol presented first is that emblematic of the Babylonish power after it had been transferred to the conjoint dynasty of the Medes and Persians.

The emblem of the Medo-Persian dynasty was a Ram with two horns of considerable and unequal height. It is unnecessary to repeat here what has already been said of the Ram when treating of the Bear. It will be sufficient to add, that Daniel saw the Medo-Persian symbol pushing westward, that is, towards Greece; northward, and southward, towards Egypt; so that no beasts or dominions could stand successfully against it. It, therefore, "did according to its will, and became great." The reason of this greatness is given in chap. xi. 1, from which we learn that it was because the kings of the Ram dynasty were strengthened by an angel-prince devoted to the interests of Judah. In the second verse of this chapter there is a particular mentioned concerning the military operations of the Ram-kings which is noted as a cause of the enmity which led in the end to the subversion of their power by the Greeks. There were thirteen Medo-Persian kings; but the revelator takes no notice of any of them after the fourth that reigned after Cyrus. In the third year of Cyrus he said to Daniel, "Behold, there shall yet stand up three kings in Persia;" namely, Cambyses, the Ahasuerus of scripture; Smerdis the Magian, and Darius: "and the fourth shall be far richer than they all." This was Xerxes: "and by his strength through his riches he shall stir up all against the realm of Grecia;" which saying is a prediction of the celebrated invasion of the west, so familiar to the reader of ancient history.

The time of the vision between this reign and the sixth year of the reign of the last of the Ram-kings, a period of about 142 years, was occupied by the prophet in considering. "And as I was considering," says he, "behold, a He Goat came from the west over the face of the whole earth;" that is, over the face of the whole Ram-empire: "and nothing upon the earth smote (him), and the Goat had a conspicuous horn between his eyes." The things represented by the Goat and its Horn are thus interpreted in the twenty-first verse of the eighth chapter: "And the rough Goat is the kingdom of Grecia: and the Great Horn between his eyes is *the first king:*" and what is affirmed of them is thus explained in chap. xi. 3: "And a mighty king shall stand up, that shall rule with great dominion, and do according to his will." The doing of this mighty king of Greece according to his will is thus expressed in chap. viii.: "And he came to the Ram, and ran unto him in the fury of his power; and he came close to him, and was moved with anger against him, and smote the Ram, and brake his two horns: and there was no power in the Ram to stand before him, but he cast him down to the ground, and stamped upon him; and there was none that could deliver the Ram out of his power." This is highly descriptive of the war between the Greeks and Persians which resulted in the overthrow of the Ram-dynasty, and the transfer of the Kingdom of Babylon to Alexander the Great, the notable horn of the goat nation. All the power of this kingdom was now vested in "the first king," who "became very great," and when he had attained to the fulness of his power, "wept because there were no more worlds for him to conquer." His dominion extended from Macedonia to beyond the Indus; and from the gulf of Persia to Scythia; and is represented by the belly of brass in Nebuchadnezzar's Image, and in the interpretation thereof termed "the third kingdom of brass which shall bear rule over all the earth."

The Ram having disappeared from view, the prophet's attention was concentrated upon the Goat, and especially upon his Horn. He saw that "when the Goat was strong, the Great Horn was broken;" that is, the power of the kingdom departed from the first king and his family before any reverses overtook the nation. Alexander died in Babylon from intoxication, leaving his unbroken dominion to be contended for and possessed by the strongest. It was revealed to Daniel that it should be divided into four notable sections, but that no blood-relations of the first king should possess them. The divisions of Alexander's empire were represented by "four notable horns coming up in the place of the broken horn toward the four winds of heaven;" and in regard to the succession it was added in chap. xi. 4, "but not to his posterity, nor according to the (extent of the) dominion which he ruled: for his kingdom shall be plucked up even for others (for other rulers) beside those" of his posterity. This is the meaning of "four kingdoms standing up out of the nation, *but not in his power.*"

The Four Heads of the Grecian Leopard, and the Four Horns of the Grecian Goat, both fours pointing toward the four winds, are representative of the same Grecian powers. The reader can refer to what I have said about the Leopard for the signification of the four horns of the Goat. In the eighth chapter nothing more is said about the four horns. They were only introduced into this vision because of the dynasty that was to succeed them as the heir of the Babylonian power, which was to make its appearance in the east "*out of one of them.*" The eleventh chapter, from the fifth to the thirty-first verse, treats of two of them, the northern and southern horns in their struggles with one another for ascendancy in the Holy Land, and consequent lordship over Judah; and thus the treatise fills up the interval between the foundation of the horn kingdoms and the incipient intervention of "the breakers of Daniel's people" who should exalt themselves to establish the vision. Besides this, two of the Goat Horns were indispensable to the representation of the solution of the Eastern Question of our day, called "the Time of the End." They are therefore introduced again in the fortieth verse; and one of them, the northern, is kept in view to the end of the chapter, being inseparable at last from the Little Horn of the Goat which came up out of it and merges again into it; so that the fate of the one becomes the fate of the other, which is to be *broken without help.*

It will be seen by the countries subjected to the third head or horn, that the Kingdom of Babylon passed from Alexander to Seleucus and his successors of the northern horn. The Babylonish power has been particularly hostile to Judah and the holy ones from Nebuchadnezzar to the present time, and will be to the end. Before Christ it seemed to have reached the climax of hatred in the reign of Antiochus Epiphanes, who polluted the temple, took away the daily, and set up the abomination of the desolator. This extreme indignation against the temple worship was *a type* of the violence of the Little Horn that should come up against Jerusalem out of his territory, the effect of which would be far more permanent than his.

In the latter time of the dominion of the northern and southern horns of the Goat the transgressors in Judah were fast arriving at maturity. The Israelites of that tribe had conquered their independence of these two kingdoms by the valor of the Maccabees and "a little help" from heaven; and in alliance with the Romans, the future breakers of their power, they were enabled to maintain it under kings of the Levitical race after they had vanished from the scene. By that time, however, both people and government had become very corrupt; so that in about a hundred years after the establishment of the Asmonean throne, when the transgressors were ripening, the Iron Men of Italy began to appear as a distinct power to the north of Judea by the progressive incorporation of the provinces of the northern horn with their more western empire. This advance of the Roman power eastward was preparatory to the use Jehovah was going to make of them in the crucifixion of Jesus, the punishment of Judah, and the abolition of the Mosaic system, as predicted in the eighth chapter, and the prophecy of the Seventy Weeks. The disappearing of the northern horn for a long series of ages, and the substituting of the Roman power in its place, was represented to Daniel by *the coming forth of a Little Horn out of one of the four horns*. After it began to appear in Syria Daniel saw it waxing exceeding great against the south or Egypt, and against the east or Euphrates, and against the glory of the land, or Palestine, until it became dangerously formidable to the army of "the heavens," or military power of Judah, which it at length subdued, as evinced by the Jews boasting before Pilate, that they had no other king than Cæsar.

Thus far the vision of the Ram and Goat was for the purpose of introducing the Roman power in its relation to Judah and the Holy Land to special notice. By the absorption of the northern kingdom into the Roman empire, a union was formed between it and the Greco-Babylonian power of the Seleucidæ; so that as these were heirs of Alexander's kingdom of Babylon, the Romans inherited it from them. Hence the power peculiar to this territory, styled "the whole earth," may very properly be called the Romano-Greek Babylonian; or the Latino-Greek Babylonian. This name is descriptive of it in its relation to the Holy Land, in all its future phases until its utter destruction by Messiah the Prince and his holy ones. The Ottoman nation is more Greek than Turkish, with but little of the Latin element; but when the Latins and Greeks come to form a confederacy under Russia as the fragile medium of combination, the Latino-Greek Babylonian power will be in full "blossom," when the sour grape is ripening for the vintage.[1] If these things be apprehended, the reader will be prepared to read the destiny of Russia and the nations in the solution of the Eastern Question; for, the working of it out is the manifestation of the Gogian Image, or Latino-Greek Babylonian power in consummation for its signal and final overthrow by the hand of God.

In this vision of the Ram and Goat the Babylonian power in its Roman manifestation is represented by *the Little Horn of the Goat*, which is not to be confounded with *the Little Horn with Eyes and Mouth*. At the time of the end, the powers signified by these are confederated with the Goat's Little Horn, and with it as their chief invade the Holy Land and besiege Jerusalem, and take it.

The Little Horn of the Goat power is described by Daniel as "a king of fierce countenance, and understanding an intricate tongue; whose power shall be mighty, but not in his own virility: and he shall destroy wonderfully, and shall prosper and work; and shall destroy multitudes, and the people of the holy ones." Speaking of the same, Moses says to Israel, "Jehovah shall bring a nation against thee from far, from the end of the earth, as the eagle flieth; a nation whose tongue thou shalt not understand; a nation of fierce countenance, which shall not regard the person of the old, nor show favor to the young. And he shall besiege thee in all thy gates, until all thy high and fenced walls come down, wherein thou trustedst throughout all thy land which Jehovah thy God hath given thee."[2] "And through

---

(1) Isai. xviii. 5; Rev. xiv. 18.   (2) Deut. xxviii. 49.

his policy also," says Daniel, "he shall cause falsehood to prosper by his power; and because of his heart he shall do proudly, and in tranquillity shall destroy many: he shall also stand up against the שַׂר־שָׂרִים Sar-sahrim, Commander of chieftains; but he shall be broken without help."

Thus in its career it was to be what is said of Daniel's fourth beast, "dreadful, and terrible, and strong exceedingly," and the special enemy of all pertaining to Judah. "It waxed great," says the prophet, "above the army of the heavens;[1] and it cast down of the army and of the stars to the ground, and stamped upon them. Yea, he magnified himself even against the שַׂר־הַצָּבָא, Sar-hatz-zahvah, Commander of the army; and by it the תָּמִיד tahmid, evening-morning sacrifice was taken away; and the מְכוֹן מִקְדָּשׁוֹ mĕkhōn mikdoshō, foundation of its temple scattered.[2] And an army was given against the evening-morning sacrifice because of rebellion, and it cast down the truth to the ground; and it wrought and prospered." This was the beginning of divine indignation against Judah in the first century of our era, which is not quite terminated yet.

10. EVENING-MORNING OBJECT.

In the twenty-sixth verse it is written, "The מַרְאֶה marai, or thing seen of the evening and morning which was told is true; wherefore shut thou up the חָזוֹן khahzōn, or vision, for it is for many days." The vision was given principally to exhibit this great object, namely, *the suppression of the evening-morning sacrifice until the Latino-Greek Babylonish power should be helplessly broken by the Commander of the army of Israel.* This is then the reason why the vision of the Ram and Goat is styled "the thing seen of the evening and morning," or the *evening-morning object.*

When Daniel had the vision, the evening and morning sacrifice was suppressed, Jerusalem in ruins, and Judah in the province of Babylon. He was, however, fondly expecting the restoration of all these in about sixteen years:[3] but here was a new vision which taught him, that a breaking up of Judah by a more formidable enemy than the Chaldeans was to occur after their restoration from the Babylonish captivity. He saw that "the Breaker up of Judah" was to exalt himself successfully against the long-expected Messiah; again to suppress the sacrifices, destroy the temple and city, abolish the Mosaic institutions, and scatter the power of the nation. In view of these events, what would become of all the promises made to the fathers of Israel? How long was deferred hope to make the hearts of believers sick? That the promises would certainly be fulfilled he had no doubt; but then, as a lover of his people, he was appalled at the greatness of their rebellion, and at the calamities it would bring upon them in punishment for their crimes. The prospect of these things had a sickening effect upon the prophet. "I fainted," said he; "and was sick for days." He had been told how long the glory of Judah should be veiled in rayless night, and that deliverance should come at last: but

---

(1) The Jewish forces are very fitly styled "the army of the heavens." These heavens were, Jehovah their king, Michael, "the first of the chief princes," styled also Michael Prince of Israel, Gabriel, and other angel-princes, appointed of God to watch over the affairs of the Jews in their relations with other powers, and so forth. Israel belongs to these heavens which rule until they give place to Messiah the prince and his holy ones, to whom God has promised to subject all things terrestrial. Israel then belonging to these heavens, their military forces are the army or host of the heavens, which must of course be sought for on the arena of the Little Horn.

(2) *Foundation of its temple* or holy place. This rendering accords with the saying, "There shall not be left here one stone upon another, that shall not be thrown down."—Matt. xxiv. 2. This would be a demolition of the foundation, and therefore utter destruction.

(3) Dan. ix. 2.

the information only left him in blank amazement; for he says, "I was astonished at the thing seen, but none understood;" that is, at what time the scattering power would be broken, and the evening and morning sacrifice restored. Though ignorant of this, Daniel had consolation in knowing that at the end of the time appointed in the vision

II. "THE HOLY SHALL BE AVENGED."

After the announcement of the all-conquering prosperity of Judah's foe, Daniel heard the question asked, "Until when the vision (*khahzōn,*) the evening-morning sacrifice (*tahmid,*) and the rebellion causing desolation, to give both the holy (*kōdesh*) and the army a treading down?" Here was an answer sought in regard to three things: *first,* Unto what period of time should the vision reach, the last incident of which is the destruction of the Latino-Greek Babylonian power? In other words, When should that destruction happen? *Secondly,* Until when should the evening-morning sacrifice be suppressed? And *thirdly,* When should Judah's rebellion, which had induced all these calamities, have an end? A fourth inquiry might be made which would cover the whole ground, namely, *How long shall the treading down of the Holy Land and the Jews continue?* Now, the answer which saluted Daniel's ears shows that the precise point of time when these things should be, cannot be extracted from the prophecy; because there is no intimation given of the commencement of the period named. The answer recorded is, "*During an evening-morning, two thousand three hundred; then the holy shall be avenged.*" The meaning of this is, that there should be an evening-morning period of 2,300 years, after the expiration of which the Holy Land should be avenged. The Lord Jesus has paraphrased the reply in these words: "Jerusalem (the holy) shall be trodden down of the Gentiles, until the times of the Gentiles be fulfilled."[1] When these have elapsed, neither Turk, Frank, nor Russian, Greek nor Latin, will be permitted to desecrate the Holy with their hateful presence and abominations; the treading down will then be terminated and the spoiler expelled; that is, when judgment is given to the holy ones at the expiration of the three times and a half.

The answer as it stands in the common version, has caused insuperable difficulties to all who have endeavored to understand it. It is rendered there, "Unto two thousand three hundred days: then shall the sanctuary be cleansed." But the original is not ימים *yahmim,* "days;" it is עֶרֶב בֹּקֶר *erev bōker,* "an evening-morning." This departure from the usual mode of expression was not without good reason. The reply was in effect, "During a two thousand three hundred *tahmid;*" that is, Judah's host for its rebellion against Jehovah was to become an evening-morning sacrifice until the end of a period of 2,300 years: as it is written, "His anger is momentary; in his favor is life; weeping may endure *for an evening;* but joy cometh *in the morning.*" This is as true of Judah as of Judah's king. And again, "A lion out of the forest (Nebuchadnezzar) shall slay them, and a wolf of the evenings shall spoil them, a leopard shall watch over their cities (the Roman Wolf and Greek Leopard,) every one that goeth out thence shall be torn in pieces; because their transgressions are many, and their backslidings are increased."[2] This was an evening sacrifice of the nation, in which they eat the bread of affliction with bitter herbs until the time of the morning oblation come, the time of Jacob's trouble,[3] when they will be avenged in the great sacrifice of Bozrah in the day of Jehovah's vengeance; and in the year of recompenses for the controversy of Zion.[4] During the suspension of the Mosaic

---

(1) Luke xxi. 24. (2) Jer. v. 6. (3) Jer. xxx. 7. (4) Isai. xxxiv. 6–8; lxiii. 1–6; Ezek. xxxix. 17.

sacrifices Judah is the *tahmid* which bleeds for its rebellion against the Lamb, slain in the evening and morning oblation from the foundation of the world.

But the phrase that has caused the greatest difficulty is, "*Then shall the sanctuary be cleansed.*" Theologists of the Gentiles have not perceived that the vision has no reference to the Gentiles but as destroyers of Judah and the enemies of their king. They have therefore imagined that "the sanctuary" to be cleansed is the Gentile church! as if any cleansing could make the thing called "the church" any thing but unclean. Assuming this, they have looked for the advent of Christ the year after the 2,300th year had expired; and have called his appearing to burn up the world, and to place those whom they style "the saints" upon the purified earth as its sole occupants in glory, "the cleansing of the sanctuary!". Well, this is as reasonable an interpretation as could be expected from people who deny the restoration of the Jews, and believe in world-burning at the coming of Christ! But so long as men hold on to such foolishness it is impossible for them to understand the Bible, or to form any rational conclusion concerning the divine predetermination respecting the issue of human affairs.

But, all speculations and absurdities connected with this subject are most readily extinguished by reference to the original. There we find that the words crucible-ized in the fires of world-burning theories do not exist! "Then shall the sanctuary be cleansed" was no part of the answer given in Daniel's hearing. The words he heard were וְנִצְדַּק קֹדֶשׁ *we-nitzdak kōdesh*. The word *kōdesh* is not "sanctuary;" but *holy;* designating *what is holy* connected with Judah, such as the Holy City, called emphatically "The Holy;" and the Holy Land. Then as to *nitzdak*, rendered *cleansed* in the common version. This is not its meaning. It signifies, *to be vindicated from injury and violence,* or to be avenged. The word for to cleanse is טִהֵר *tahhar*, and is used several times in the sense of to cleanse Judea from the putrefying bodies of the slain in the prophecy of the Autocrat of Russias' overthrow in the breaking of the Latino-Greek Babylonian power.¹ "*Then the Holy shall be avenged,*" is the only proper rendering of which the original is susceptible in this place. Let it be also observed, that this does not teach that the avenging of the holy is to commence immediately the 2300th evening-morning is finished. It only gives us to understand that when that period is passed, the next *series* of events in relation to the Holy Land shall be *the manifestation of things necessary to wrest it from the Gentiles, and to avenge it in their overthrow.*

It must be evident to every intelligent reader, that, before a country in the actual possession of an enemy can be avenged for its desolations of twenty-three hundred years, *a situation of affairs must be created favoring its deliverance.* This requires time; and the time provided in the case before us is styled, "*the time of the end,*" now current. Every year since 1840 the Holy Land has been mixing itself up more and more with the policy of the Gentile Powers; until at the present time a situation of affairs in the east is nearly formed which will make its possession by other powers than the Ottoman a matter of belligerent dispute. Here are fourteen years consumed in bringing affairs to their present crisis, which is by no means ripe enough for the accomplishment of the prediction, "*the Holy shall be avenged.*" The overthrow of the Latino-Greek Babylonian Dragon under the supremacy of the Czar on the mountains of Israel is indispensable to this most desirable consummation.

The reply to the question "*Until when?*" did not state the *anno mundi* as the terminus, but the development of a work. One step, however, was gained towards a solution of the question, and that was, that whenever the beginning of the period might be, the avenging of the holy would not be short of 2300 years afterwards.

---

(1) Ezek. xxxix. 12, 14, 16.

Daniel had the vision B. C. 554, which is 2866 years ago. This was a long period to look forward to the end of; and by no method of calculation could he reduce it to less than 2300 years. Happily for us, if of Daniel's class, we live after its termination. We know its beginning and end; but neither can be ascertained from the eighth chapter. "The vision is for many days," whose commencement was not revealed to Daniel until the first year of Darius the Mede, sixteen years after, as narrated in the

12. PROPHECY OF THE SEVENTY WEEKS.

About fifteen years after beholding the vision of the Ram and Goat, Daniel's mind was particularly attracted to the subject of the restoration of Judah and Jerusalem.[1] The seventy years divinely appointed for the continuance of the Chaldean dynasty of the kingdom of Babylon had expired, and with them its last king had fallen. Judah's destroyer had been punished, and Daniel, instructed by Jeremiah, began to look for his people's deliverance. Isaiah informed him that one Koresh, or Cyrus, should appear as a shepherd of Jehovah, and perform his pleasure, "Even saying to Jerusalem, Thou shalt be built; and to the temple, Thy foundation shall be laid."[2] With this Cyrus thus named so long before his birth, Daniel, was now personally acquainted. The first year of Darius the Mede had come, and with it the 68th year of the prophet's exile from Judea. He was aware that the Holy Land was to rest ten heptades, or seventy years; he could not therefore but be singularly interested in the times, for only two years were wanting to their completion. At last they too had passed away. After reigning two years his friend Darius died, and was succeeded by his nephew Cyrus; and Daniel had the satisfaction of reading his proclamation for the return of Judah, and the rebuilding of the temple.

Under the full and lively expectation of the restoration of his people, Daniel confessed with deep and sincere repentance the rebellion for which they had been righteously punished through the Chaldeans; and besought Jehovah that he would turn away his anger and fury from his city Jerusalem, his holy mountain; and cause his face to shine upon his sanctuary מִקְדָּשׁ *mikdôsh*, then in ruins, for his own sake; seeing that the people and the city were called by his name.

While he was yet speaking in prayer, Gabriel appeared to him at the time of the evening sacrifice. Fifteen or sixteen years before, Gabriel had been authorized to make Daniel understand the vision concerning the *tahmid*, or evening-morning sacrifice.[3] But as we have seen, he only accomplished this to a limited extent. He had left Daniel "astonished at the vision, but none understood." He saw the destruction of the people of the holy ones; the greatness of their destroyer's power; his presumption in contending in battle with their Commander-in-Chief; and his final overthrow: but of the beginning of the vision's many days, and of what was to occur in relation to Messiah the Prince, *before* the taking away of the evening and morning sacrifice, and the casting down of the foundation of the temple—of these things he had no understanding. Gabriel was therefore sent a second time "to make him skilful of understanding," that he might "discern the word" he then brought to him, "and understand the thing seen (*marai*)," in respect to the evening-morning, or *tahmid*, rendered "the daily."

Having directed Daniel's attention to their last interview, Gabriel proceeded to declare "the word" he had received as a key to the 2300 evening and morning exhibition. The following is a

---

(1) Dan. ix.   (2) Isai. xliv. 28; Ezra, 1.   (3) Dan. viii. 16.

13. CORRECTED VERSION OF THE PROPHECY.

24. Seventy heptades are cut off[1] relatively to thy people and to thine Holy City for perfecting the rebellion, and for making sin-offerings complete; and for expiating iniquity, and for bringing in the righteousness of the ages, and for sealing a vision and prophet, and for anointing the Holy One of holy ones. 25. Know therefore and understand: from the issuing of a command for a restoring and for building Jerusalem unto the Anointed One the Prince Royal, shall be seven heptades, and sixty and two heptades: she shall return and be built; the broad wall and the breach in straitness of the times. 26. And after the sixty and two heptades the Anointed shall be put to death, though nothing will be in him; and the Prince Royal's people who shall come shall destroy the City and the Holy (Land), the end thereof being as a flood; and unto the end of the war desolations are decreed.

27. And He shall confirm a covenant for many one heptade; and in the half of the heptade he shall cause to desist from sacrifice and oblation; and with an overspreading of abominations make desolate even to the consummation; but that decreed shall be poured out upon that which is to be destroyed.

In the twenty-fourth verse Daniel learned that there were six particulars to become accomplished facts before an army should be given to the Romano-Greek Babylonian Little Horn against the evening and morning sacrifice for the suppression of it, and the destruction of the holy city and people, and the consequent abolition of the Mosaic law and constitution. These important particulars may be thus ordinally presented:

1. The perfecting of Judah's rebellion;
2. The making sin-offerings complete;
3. The expiating of iniquity;
4. The bringing in the righteousness for the ages;
5. The sealing a vision and prophet;
6. The anointing the Holy One of holy ones.

1. In chap. viii. the reason assigned for the standing up of the "King of a fierce countenance" against Judah in the latter time of the northern and southern kingdoms of the Goat is, "so as to cause transgressors to fill up their measure," which I take to be the meaning of כהתם הפשעים *kh' hahthaim haph-pohshim*, rendered in the English version, "when the transgressors are come to the full." This is not true in fact. The transgressors in Judah had not filled up their measure in the latter time of the reign of the Kings of Syria and Egypt, when the Roman power stood up in their place against Judah. This is evident from the Lord's denunciations in which he said to them a hundred years after, "Fill ye up then the measure of your fathers, ye hypocrites."[2] The Roman power was allowed to overshadow Judah as a means of bringing their rebellion against Jehovah to a head, or to perfect it, according to Gabriel. Every reader of the apostolic writings must be familiar with the way this was accomplished. The Lord Jesus appeared among them as "THE HEIR" of the Kingdom and throne of David; and they said, "Come, let us kill him, and let us seize on his inheritance."[3] They arraigned him before the tribunal of the Little Horn on a charge of high treason against it, because he claimed to be King of the Jews, and therefore spoke against the imperial rights of Cæsar. But Pontius Pilate, the Horn's representative in Judea, apprehending no danger,

---

(1) The original is *nekhthak*, and found only in this place in the Hebrew Scriptures; more commonly in Chaldee and Rabbinic.
(2) Matt. xxiii. 32.   (3) Matt. xxi. 38.

would have acquitted him with release, knowing that for envy they had delivered him. But he could prevail nothing; for the rebels cried out, saying, "If thou let this man go thou art not Cæsar's friend; whosoever maketh himself a King, speaketh against Cæsar." "Behold your King!" said the governor. "Away with him, away with him," they cried; "crucify him!" The astonished Pilate exclaimed, "Shall I crucify your King?" But, "the Chief Priest answered, We have no King but Cæsar." Thus was the first particular of Gabriel's word accomplished. Judah's rebellion was perfected within a few hours of the expiration of the seventy times seven years from the passover of the 20th year of the reign of Artaxerxes, Ram-king of Babylon.

2. The next thing was to make sin-offerings complete. This did not mean to put a stop to the evening-morning sacrifice; for that was not effected till about thirty-five years after the end of the seventy heptades. It was to make them complete in relation to those who should partake in the righteousness to be brought in through the expiation for iniquity. We read of no more sin-offerings being presented by the apostles, who had been made clean through the word spoken to them by Jesus; nor did they enjoin sin-offerings upon those who received their teaching. "By the" Abrahamic or "Second Will, they were sanctified through the offering of *the body* of Jesus Christ once;" "for by one offering he hath perfected for ever them that are sanctified:" so that, having thus obtained a permanent remission, "no more offering for sin" was needed. Hence they were made completed in Messiah's antitypical Expiation though they continued to be offered by the rebels.

3. A third item to be accomplished before the passing away of the seventy heptades, or periods of seven years, was the *expiating of iniquity*. The verb rendered *to expiate* is khahphar, to cover, or overlay, to hide. Hence, khaphporeth, a cover, and therefore applied to the cover of the Ark of the Testimony in the Most Holy Place of the Temple, called the Propitiatory, because propitiation or expiation was made for sin by sprinkling it with the blood of the sacrifices. 'It was also called THE MERCY SEAT. A good conscience is without shame or fear. Transgression of law, or sin, converts a good conscience into a bad one, and developes shame and fear. Before he sinned, Adam's conscience was good; he was naked, but not at all ashamed, or afraid of the presence of the Elohim: but immediately after, his conscience being defiled, shame and fear caused him *to hide* himself, because he was *uncovered*. This teaches us that *sin needs to be covered*. Adam felt this, and undertook *to cover his own sin* in the best way he could devise, being ignorant of the manner in which sin is covered by divine appointment. But the Lord God stripped him of his own device, which did not recognize the principle of blood-shedding in the covering of iniquity. He taught Adam *to shed the blood of a lamb, and to cover his nakedness with its skin*. This was the lamb slain *at* "the foundation of the world," and represented him who is the Lamb typically slain *from* the foundation of the world. Adam and his wife were in this way clothed by the Lord God; and being thus clothed, their iniquity was expiated or covered.

The only Sin-Covering from the Fall to the resurrection of Jesus, the world had ever known, was typical; or a yearly covering of sin that represented the covering foretold by Gabriel. The patriarchs, prophets, and others, who Abrahamically believed the things covenanted to the fathers, and were dead, had died with no other covering for their sins than could be derived from the pouring out of the blood of bulls and goats. But "It is not possible that the blood of bulls and of goats should take away sins;"[1] their sins therefore remained uncovered and unexpiated; and as "the wages of sin is death," if the expiation of the seventy heptades had never been effected, they would never have risen from the dead to eternal life. Hence, speaking of the completing efficacy of Christ's death, Paul says, "For this

(1) Heb. x. 4.

cause he is the Mediator of the New (or Abrahamic) Covenant, that by means of death *for the redemption of the transgressions under the first covenant* (the Law) that they which are called might receive the promise of the everlasting inheritance:"[1] and Isaiah says, "For the transgression of my people was he stricken." Thus, the death and resurrection of the Mediator, and therefore Representative Testator, of the Covenant made with Abraham, brought it into force; so that the already dead who had while living believed the things promised in it, obtained a covering of their sins, the effect of which they will experience on rising from the dead to possess them for the age.

4. If Messiah the Prince had not been cut off for his people of all ages, "*righteousness for the ages*," the fourth item of Gabriel's word, could not have been "*brought in*." Faith in the things of the Kingdom could not have been counted for righteousness to life in the future ages of glory, without a propitiatory or mercy seat, sprinkled with blood. The cutting off of Jesus provided this indispensable *kaphporeth*, or cover for sin: so that he being slain and raised from the dead, the means of a sinner's justification, styled, "The righteousness of God," was brought in or completed within the period appointed.

Here then were the victim and the covering provided by Jehovah—*a victim of expiation for the sins of the faithful;* the faithful who believed the promises covenanted to Abraham and David:—*a covering garment to hide their sins* in putting on the victim by immersion into his name. Thus invested or clothed upon, they are in Christ, who of God becomes to them thus, "wisdom, and righteousness, and sanctification, and redemption."

When these things should be effected, sin-offerings, and the evening-morning sacrifices, which were merely typical, could well be dispensed with. In relation then to the taking away of the *tahmid*, and the destruction of the holy city, Daniel would perceive their accomplishment posterior to the fulness of the seventy heptades of years. Hence all those speculations that make Antiochus the Little Horn, and his oppression of the Jews, and defilement of the temple, and so forth, the fulfilment of chap. viii. 11, 23, 24, are entirely inadmissible, and altogether unworthy of a grave or respectful attention.

5. The fifth particular to come to pass before the passing away of the heptades was *the sealing of a vision and a prophet*. If the sealing had related to that seen of Daniel in the third of Belshatzar the article *the* would have preceded *vision* in the text. We are informed that in the early days of Samuel, "The word of the Lord was precious;" for there was no open vision; and in Jeremiah it is said "They speak a vision of their own heart." To speak the word of the Lord is for a prophet to speak what the Lord impresses upon his brain. We perceive before we speak; hence, to reveal our perceptions is to speak what we see, or, *to speak a vision*. When a man speaks impressions made upon him by the Lord, and the Lord confirms what he speaks, he speaks *an open vision*, and the confirmation is *the sealing* of it. "Bind together the testimony; seal instruction among my disciples." This was done in the ministrations of the Lord Jesus. He spoke an open vision, instructing his disciples; and his instructions the Father sealed, by the signs and wonders that accompanied them.

In sealing the vision of the seventieth heptade, the prophet by whom the vision was spoken, was sealed likewise. The confirmation of the vision was the confirmation of its prophet also. "Believe me," said Jesus, "for the works' sake." In another place, he says, "The Father himself, who hath sent me, hath borne witness of me. Have ye never heard his voice nor seen his form?"—the voice from the excellent glory, and the form of the dove? Multitudes had seen this, and were compelled to say, "This is of a truth that prophet that should come into the world." The sealing of the vision and the prophet go together, and are therefore

---

(1) Heb. ix. 15.

placed together in Gabriel's word; and have unquestionable reference to Jesus, who speaking of himself says, "Him has the Father sealed."

6. The sixth and last of Gabriel's specifications in this verse is *the anointing a Holy One of Saints*. This personage was the Messiah, a name signifying *an anointed one*. There have been many anointed ones, but the one here referred to was to be preëminently such; and to be anointed within the limits of the seventieth heptade; that is, sometime between the end of the sixty-ninth and the end of the seventieth, as appears from verse 25. Believing that Jesus is Messiah the Prince, we are at no loss where to place the anointing. Peter says, "God anointed Jesus of Nazareth with the Holy Spirit and with power;" and Luke, after relating the particulars concerning it, says, that "Jesus himself began to be about thirty years of age."[1] This fixes the baptism and anointing at *five years and three months* before the crucifixion. Thus, "God anointed him with the oil of gladness *above* his associates."[2] He is therefore the Holy One of those holy associates, or the Holy One of holy ones, as I have rendered the text.

Having specified these six things to be accomplished before the expiration of the seventy heptades, Gabriel proceeded to specify the commencement of them. He stated that to *Mashiach Nahgid*, the Anointed Prince, should be "seven heptades, and threescore and two heptades," that is, sixty-nine. This period extended to the *proclamation* of Messiah the Prince being at hand; that is, to the beginning of John's preaching, who said that he came baptizing in water that He might be made manifest to Israel,[3] which manifestation is styled "His coming."[4] Sixty-nine heptades of years calculated from this announcement gives 483 years, and nine months; that is, it carries us up to the twentieth year of the reign of Artaxerxes, Persian King of Babylon, when Nehemiah, his cup-bearer, received commandment to go and restore and build Jerusalem, and set up the wall. How Nehemiah executed this work is fully detailed in the portion of scripture that passes by his name.

This commandment of Artaxerxes did not issue till 84 years after Gabriel's visit to Daniel, who would, therefore, still be ignorant of the commencement of the "many days" of the vision he had seen in the third year of Belshatzar's reign. He would understand that the 2,300 and the seventy Heptades began at the issuing of the commandment; but when that authorization for the restitution of Jerusalem and the Wall should be granted, he could not, and, it is probable, that even Gabriel himself was unable, to tell. All they knew was, that it would be 483 years to the proclamation of repentance, because Messiah the Prince was in the midst of Israel, and about to appear; but whether 483 years from the first year of Cyrus, or from a hundred years afterwards, they did not know.

It may be remarked here, that there were *four decrees*, or commands, promulged by kings of the Ram Dynasty, in favor of Judah and Jerusalem. The first was in the first year of Cyrus, two years after Gabriel's visit; and authorized the Jews to return to Palestine and rebuild the temple.[5] This was 70 years after Jehoiakim's rebellion against Nebuchadnezzar, in the third of Cyrus's reign; and B. C. 538.

The *second decree*[6] was issued by Darius the Persian, sixteen years after; that is, in the second of his reign, enforcing that of Cyrus, being 70 years from the burning of the temple, in the 19th of Nebuchadnezzar, B. C. 522. The temple was finished four years afterwards, in the sixth of his reign,[7] answering to 70 years from the 23d of Nebuchadnezzar, when 745 persons were carried captive to Babylon.

The *third decree* was promulgated in the 7th of Artaxerxes, for the restoration of the Commonwealth of Judah.[8] This was 53 years after the temple was finished, and 71 from the decree of Cyrus.—B. C. 467.

---

(1) Luke iii. 23; Acts x. 38. (2) Psalms xlv. 7. (3) John i. 31. (4) Acts xiii. 24.
(5) Ezra 1. (6) Ezra vi. 1. (7) Ezra vi 15. (8) Ezra vii. 7, 11–26.

The *fourth decree* was thirteen years after, in the 20th of Artaxerxes, B. C. 454 years and 9 months. This was for the building of the broad wall and the setting up of the gates of Jerusalem.[1]

From these chronological data the reader will perceive, that the last decree is the only one from which the first Seventy Heptades of the 2,300 evening and morning, or day of Judah's trouble, can reasonably be commenced; for the others all fall short of the proclamation of "the King of the Heavens having approached" by many years. The 20th of Artaxerxes may, therefore, be regarded as the established *terminus à quo*, or point of departure in the calculation of the time.

It is proper, however, to mention that the usual reckoning of the B. C.. answering to the 20th Artaxerxes, is 445 years. This would make the end of the 69 heptades three years after the crucifixion; and removing this event seven years later, as happening at the end of the 70th heptade. But by reference to my chronology at the end of Elpis Israel, it will be found that the numbers indicating the duration of the reigns placed opposite the kings, and which I culled out of Rollin's History, between the 20th Artaxerxes and the birth of Jesus, make exactly 454 years and 9 months. From the birth to the baptism (on the authority of Luke,) was 30 years, making 484 and 9 months. This was 1 year and 9 months after the end of the 69th Heptade; and consequently so far advanced into the seventieth. But the common reckoning is flagrantly erroneous in divers places, and of no authority where critical accuracy is desired.

Having indicated the beginning and ending of the 69 heptades, and divided them into successive portions of seven heptades and sixty-two heptades, Gabriel informed Daniel that the Messiah should be cut off after the sixty-two heptades had passed away. But, at this part of the revelation he did not tell him, how soon after their termination the cutting off should transpire. He informed him, furthermore, that after the cutting off, destruction should come upon the City and the Holy by a people of the Prince, and that at the end of the destruction there should be a flood of evil, and unto an end of the war desolations were decreed. The cutting off, the destruction, and the desolations, were consecutive events, but not immediately so. Between the cutting off of Messiah and the destruction of the City and Holy were about thirty-eight years, and between the city's overthrow and the war of the Romans against Barchochebas, was upwards of forty. This last war completely prostrated them. They had massacred hundreds of thousands of Greeks and Egyptians in cold blood; at length the Little Horn "*stamped upon them*," after causing a loss to Judah of 580,000 on the field of battle in two years.

Having extended Daniel's view to the destruction of the people of the Saints, by the Little Horn power,[2] that is, by the host or army that was given to it[3] by the Prince, or Messiah,[4] against the rebels and the *tahmid*, Gabriel recalled his attention to the last of the Seventy Heptades; and informed him what the work was that should be accomplished by the Prince in the course of that seven years, from 483 to 490 of the period. "He shall confirm a covenant for many in the course of one heptade; and in half of the heptade he shall cause to desist from sacrifice and oblation." The covenant to be confirmed was the New, or Abrahamic, Covenant. This had been *typically* confirmed of God, concerning Christ, 430 years before the night of the departure from Egypt. Abraham's sacrifices which were consumed by fire from heaven, represented, or pointed to, the cutting off of Messiah, the Prince, as *the* sacrifice, whose blood is the blood of the Covenant "shed for many." On the night on which he was betrayed, while eating the Passover with his disciples, Jesus said, "*I even I am covenanted for you as my Father covenants for me a kingdom, in order that ye may eat and drink at my table in my kingdom, and may sit upon thrones, judging the Twelve Tribes of Israel.*"[5] He was made a covenant in

---

(1) Neh. ii. 1.   (2) Dan. viii. 24.   (3) Dan. viii. 12.
(4) Matt. xxii. 7.   (5) Luke xxii. 29, 30.

being cut off as an expiation for the sins of Abraham and his heirs; and in so dying, to bring the covenant made for them into force. That covenant, or will, was like all other wills, which are of no force while the testator liveth. Messiah, the Prince, being the Mediatorial Testator, Jehovah's representative in the affair, was the confirmer of the covenant for its many heirs; for if he had not voluntarily surrendered himself to death, all the work of the previous seven years would have been null and void. In dying and rising again he made it sure, having dedicated it with his blood. This is, therefore, the antitypical blood of the Abrahamic covenant, to the things of which all are entitled *who believe them*, and whose hearts have been sprinkled with it. It is for them the Prince confirmed the covenant with his own blood. They are the "many" referred to by Gabriel, Daniel and the prophets, and so forth, among the number. "*I will give thee,*" saith Jehovah, in prophecy to his Son, "*for a covenant of the people, to establish the land, to cause to possess the desolate estates.*"[1] The promise of this gift was redeemed in the gift of a son to Israel,[2] and the acceptance of him as the covenant purifier of his brethren. The covenant being confirmed, then, the land promised to Abraham and his Seed, and to all in them, will assuredly become the dwelling-place of glory, and they will possess it with all that is requisite to make it "the inheritance of the saints in light."

The phrase *khatzi hasshahvua* is very incorrectly rendered "in the midst of the week" in the English version. It is the accusative of time how long, and not *a precise point* of time. *Khatzi* signifies *one-half*, or one division of the whole seven years. Daniel was not informed which of the equal divisions of the last heptade was to witness the desisting from sacrifice and oblation, by divine authority. He might infer that it would be the end of the latter half of the heptade, as the causing to desist was the last incident revealed, included in the whole seventy sevens, or heptades of years. He might conclude that Messiah, the Prince, would not cause to desist from sacrifice and oblation till expiation were made for iniquity, and righteousness for the ages were brought in. This conclusion would have been correct; still he was left to inference, as Gabriel did not satisfy him on the point. We, however, are not left to inference. The prediction being long since an accomplished fact, we know that the *khatzi* referred to is the latter part of the seventieth heptade, and on the last day thereof, that is, of the crucifixion, which was exactly 490 years, or Seventy Heptades, from the month Nisan of the 20th of Artaxerxes, B. C. 454.

The verb *shahvath*, rendered *cause to cease* in the common version, signifies *to desist* as well as *to cease*. The common rendering has puzzled all who have attempted an interpretation of the text. Some have assumed that the Prince who sends his army to destroy the city is Titus; others, that he is Antiochus; and that consequently, as no personage is introduced into the text after him, Titus, or Antiochus, is the confirmer of the covenant, and the causer of the sacrifice and oblation to cease, when they took away the daily!! Moses Stuart, that Prince of Blind Guides, says, it was "Antiochus dictated the firm league between himself and the Jewish apostates!" This is his interpretation of "He shall confirm a covenant for many." But I will not waste time, ink, and paper, in refuting such nonsense; I will only add, that he says, Antiochus caused the sacrifice and the oblation to cease by violence over 160 years before Christ; while others affirm that Titus did it 73 years after his birth. These opinions result from a supposition, that *causing the sacrifice and oblation to cease* is the same thing as *taking away the daily*. But as we have seen, they are totally different events. The former was to happen within the 490 years; while for the latter, "no man knew the day and hour, no, not the angels which are in heaven, neither the Son, but the Father."[3] Jesus, the Prince of the future kings of the earth, causing to desist from sacrifice and oblation

---

(1) Isai. xlix. 8.   (2) Isai. ix. 6.   (3) Mark xiii. 32.

is intelligible, in keeping with the time, and with the doctrine of the apostles, through which he caused all his disciples no longer to seek expiation and righteousness by the law and institutions of Moses.

A doctrine being introduced which was calculated to cause those of Judah, who received it, to desist from sacrifice and oblation, the seventy sevens of years were fully accomplished. What now remained were the "*days of vengeance*, that all things which were written might be fulfilled."[1] The vengeance was "the judgment to come" on Judah, because of their having perfected their rebellion in rejecting Jesus as their king, and putting him to death. The city and the holy nation, their constitution and country, were to be desolated by an overspreading destruction, which was to prevail without mitigation until the end of the 2,300, after which preparation would be made for the avenging of the holy. This decree is expressed in those words of Gabriel, which have so puzzled and confounded all the critics, contained in the last verse of the ninth chapter. I will quote them as they ought to read, "And with an overspreading of abominations make desolate even until the consummation, and that decreed shall be poured out upon that to be destroyed." The thing to be destroyed when the desolation shall be consummated is the "king of fierce countenance, *who shall stand up against the sar-sahrim*," or Commander in Chief of Judah, which shall be broken by him, and so come to his end, with none to help him in a "time of trouble such as never was since there was a nation to that same time."[2]

Since the "days of vengeance" which came upon Judah thirty-eight years after the ending of the seventy weeks, various "abominations" have rested like a כָּנָף *kĕnaph* upon the land. These have all been of a desolating character, such as the Romano-Greek, Persian, Saracen, and Ottoman abominations. Hence they have been כְּנַף שִׁקּוּצִים *kĕnaph shikkutzim*, an overspreading of abominations, מְשֹׁמֵם *mĕshōmaim*, making desolate. The holy is under this covering still. The 1290 years of abomination, the greater part of which has been Moslem, have passed away; and "that decreed" has been "pouring out" upon its desolator, as Gabriel foretold. The Turk is the desolator pertaining to the Moslem abomination that still overspreads the Holy Land; and the day of his destruction has arrived. The sixth vial has been pouring out upon him since 1820, and is visibly pouring upon him at this juncture. But when he goes down to the sides of the pit the Russianized Latino-Greek Babylonian power will invade the land under Gog, the king of the north, and encamp against the Holy Mountain. The consummating judgments of the sixth vial will then fall upon him as the latter-day representative of the Little Horn of the Goat. His fate is therefore that of the fierce king, as Ezekiel hath described it.

14. "MESSIAH THE PRINCE."

It may be in place here briefly to consider the titles given to the chieftain in this prophecy who is to deliver Judah, and break the adversary in pieces. In the eighth chapter he is designated by two titles; the one, שַׂר־הַצָּבָא *Sar-hatz-zahvah*, Commander of the army; and the other, שַׂר־שָׂרִים *Sar-sahrim*, Commander of commanders, or Commander in Chief of the army. In the seventh chapter, the Son of Man and the holy ones, and their people, are introduced upon the arena of the Dragon-power, with judgment given to them for its destruction; but the military relation they were to sustain towards one another in the work, though it might be inferred, was not expressed. In the chapter before us, however, this deficiency is supplied: the Son of Man is styled Commander in Chief; the holy ones, Commanders; and their people, the army of the heavens. Thus, a military

---

(1) Luke xxi. 22.   (2) Dan. viii. 23–25; xi. 45; xii. 1.

power is prospectively prepared for the work of destroying the armies of the Gentiles when, as in the days of Joshua, Israel shall be commissioned to go up and possess the Holy Land, and to subdue the kingdoms of the west.

The Bible is full of testimony to this effect, which in the New Testament is pictorially illustrated. There the Commander in Chief is represented as a King and General riding a white horse, clothed with a vesture dipped in blood, and a sharp sword going out of his mouth, that with it he should smite the nations. This symbol is declared to be representative of the King of kings, and Lord of lords, who judges and makes war in righteousness, and treads the winepress of the fierceness and wrath of Almighty God.[1] In another chapter, he is styled "*the Lamb.*" Speaking of the papal kings of the west, the Spirit says: "These shall make war with the Lamb, and the Lamb shall overcome them: for he is Lord of lords, and King of kings."[2] As to the person represented by the Lamb, he is defined as one that had been slain, and had redeemed his companion kings and lords from Israel and the nations.[3] No person intelligent in the Scriptures can deny that *these symbols are representative of Jesus Christ in the character of a Royal Military Commander in active service against the armies of the Gentiles.* The *white horse* that bears the Conquering Hero is Judah; and the "sword going forth from his mouth" is Ephraim, or the Ten Tribes of Israel with them; as is proved by the following testimonies: "Jehovah of armies hath visited the house of Judah, and hath made them *as his goodly horse* in the battle: and they shall be as mighty men who tread down their enemies in the mire of the streets in the battle; and they shall fight, *because the Lord is with them.*"[4] "Israel is Jehovah's inheritance: therefore thus saith the Lord, Thou art my battle-axe and weapons of war; for with thee will I break in pieces the nations, and with thee will I destroy kingdoms; with thee will I break in pieces captains and rulers."[5] "Behold, I will make thee a new sharp threshing instrument having teeth; thou shalt thresh the mountains, and beat them small, and shalt make the hills as chaff. Thou shalt fan them, and the wind shall carry them away, and the whirlwind shall scatter them: and thou shalt rejoice in Jehovah, and shalt glory in the Holy One of Israel."[6] "I will render double unto thee when I have bent Judah for me, filled the (Judah) bow with Ephraim, (as the arrow,) and raised up thy sons, O Zion, against thy sons, O Greece, and made thee (Zion) *as the sword of a mighty man.* And the Lord shall be seen over them, and his arrow (Ephraim) shall go forth as the lightning: and the Lord God shall blow the trumpet, and shall go forth as whirlwinds of the south."[7]

In these testimonies there are things affirmed that have never come to pass since they were written. Judah has never been since then Jehovah's goodly horse in the battle, fighting because the Lord was with them, and seen over them. Instead of Israel breaking in pieces the nations, destroying kingdoms, and reducing the empires of the Gentiles to chaff, they have been themselves the broken and destroyed. What is here testified remains to be accomplished in the *simultaneous* breaking to pieces of the gold, the silver, the brass, the iron, and the clay, of Nebuchadnezzar's Image; and the reducing them to the likeness of the chaff of the summer threshing-floors: and in the overcoming of the armies of the Beast and the kings of the Latino-Greek dominion. In this war, which will be the last on the Babylonian earth for a thousand years, "*Israel will do valiantly*"[8] as the goodly horse and sword of the Mighty One, as represented in the apocalypse of John.

The *commanders* of whom the Lord Jesus is the royal chief, are represented as his body-guards, or staff, in the apocalyptic vision. They are there styled "τα στρατευματα, *ta strateumata*, the body-guards in the heaven that follow him upon

---

(1) Rev. xix. 11–16. (2) Rev. xvii. 14. (3) Rev. v. 6–10. (4) Zech. x. 3–5.
(5) Jer. li. 19–23. (6) Isai. xli. 15, 16. (7) Zech. ix. 13, 14. (8) Numb. xxiv. 18.

white horses, clothed in fine linen, white, and clean." As they are his associate commanders of Judah, their king's goodly horse, they are fitly represented as all riding horses similar to his. The Commander in Chief's vesture is dipped in human blood; because before the things represented in the nineteenth chapter, he had "trodden the winepress *alone*, and stained all his raiment" at Bozrah,"[1] when he shatters the Russo-Gogian Image into fragmental parts, previous to "breaking them to pieces *together*." After the overthrow at Bozrah, he prepares to subdue the West; and in this preparation he summons his companions in arms to the conflict as commanders of Israel. Not having been in battle before since their resurrection, their vestments are unstained with the blood of the enemy, and therefore represented simply as emblematic of their character. To be clothed in "*fine linen, white and clean*," is significative of the wearer's righteousness. This is the interpretation put upon the symbolic raiment in the eighth verse of this chapter; for, speaking of these holy ones as constituents of the Bride ready for union with the Lamb, it is there written: "To her was granted that she should be arrayed in fine linen, clean and white; for the fine linen is (or represents) the righteousness of the holy ones." They therefore who are represented as clothed with this figurative raiment are the holy ones spoken of in Daniel; and prepared to go forth with Jesus to judge and make war in righteousness. They are the lords and kings of whom he is the Lord and King—"the called, and chosen, and faithful that are with him;"[2] the "redeemed from among men, who follow him whithersoever he goeth."[3]

In the ninth of Daniel, as we have seen, this great commander of heaven's forces against the Russianized Greco-Latin confederacy occupying the Holy Land, is styled the Holy One of holy ones, which is equivalent to the Most Holy of them. He was to be anointed by the Spirit of Jehovah, which was done at his immersion in the Jordan. He was therefore the Anointed Most Holy One of God, who had constituted him the heir of the throne of His kingdom of Israel. For this cause he is styled מָשִׁיחַ נָגִיד *mahshiaoh nahgid*, the anointed prince royal; or as in the common version, MESSIAH THE PRINCE. In the twenty-sixth verse in one sentence he is termed the Anointed One; and in another simply *nahgid*, or prince royal. In the Syriac version, "the anointed prince royal" is expressed by "the Anointed One the King," as though it were *melekh* instead of *nahgid*. But, I conceive, that there is all the difference between *melekh* and *nahgid* as that existing between the heir-apparent and the king upon his throne. Till the Anointed One ascends the throne of his father David he is Prince Royal, or king expectant, not king in fact. It must be so; for a *melekh*, or king, is *one who reigns*, and not one who expects to reign. This distinction is maintained by Jesus himself in the twenty-sixth of Matthew. In the thirty-first of that chapter, when speaking of his appearing in glory to sit upon the throne of his glory, he styles himself simply "the Son of Man;" but when he possesses that throne, and invites the blessed of the Father to occupy the kingdom in verse 34, he terms himself "the King."

But, if *Sar* mean "prince," in the sense in which the Son of Man is a prince royal, as the common version has it for *nagidh*, נָשִׂיא *nahsi*, as well as *sar*, why is he not styled *the anointed Sar?* If the revelator did not intend to convey distinct ideas concerning the Son of Man, I do not see why these three words should be all applied to him. King James' translators discerned no reason for the employment of these various words; so they rendered them all by the one word, "*prince*." But I see no reason to follow their example. I take it rather that there was design in the variety; each word being adapted to the Son of Man in the part he was represented as enacting at the time; thus, while breaking the Russo-Gogian con-

(1) Isai. lxiii. 1-4.   (2) Rev. xvii. 14.   (3) Rev. xiv. 1-5.

federacy he is called *Sar;* when making expiation for iniquity his military character is veiled, and he is styled the anointed most holy one, or *nahgid;* and when elevated to the throne in Israel, he is termed *nahsi:* so that a *sar* anointed becomes a *nahgid;* and a *nahgid* elevated to his throne a *nahsi.*

This verbal criticism is in harmony with after developments. At the end of the sixty-nine heptades, or 483 years, John the Immerser heralded the approaching manifestation of a royal personage, a *nahgid*, not of a military commander, or *Sar;* but of the future majesty of the kingdom of the heavens. The Son of Man was to appear as the rightful claimant of David's throne and the Holy Land; that is, to establish his right to it; not to gather Israel to his standard at that time for a contest with the Latino-Greek Little Horn, then "waxed exceeding great." The time had not come for that, as he told Pontius Pilate. He came, not only to prove his claim, but to bring the Abrahamic Covenant into force by his death and resurrection; that by virtue of it he might afterwards rightfully lay hold of the sovereignty of Israel and the nations, and compel the latter by the edge of the sword to recognize him as king of all the earth. No other conqueror by whom he will have been preceded since the days of Nimrod will have been able to prove his right to universal dominion by virtue of a legal instrument divinely attested and confirmed. Their right has been derived from their own swords; and they have reigned on the principle of "might is right; therefore keep who can." Israel's Commander in Chief claims all existing dominions by right derived from God; and proclaims his intention to meet them upon their own principle, and laying hold upon them with a strong arm, to wrest from them their thrones, and to keep them by his might.

Had Gabriel told Daniel that it should be 483 years to the anointed one the *Sar,* he would perhaps have expected him in the capacity of a military chieftain within the 490 years; and then, if Gabriel had added, the Anointed One shall be cut off, or "slain," as the Syriac has it, he might have inferred, that he would be slain in battle: but when he heard that he was to be put to death as prince royal, he would understand that it was in connection with the question of his right to the royalty, as we learn it really was from the testimony of Matthew, Mark, Luke, and John. He was put to death as prince royal, not as *Sar*—as heir of David, and therefore Israel and Judah's king.

Speaking of the prince, Gabriel said, "The people of the prince that shall come shall destroy the city and the holy." This refers to the "days of vengeance," or "judgment to come," preached by the apostles; and referred to by Jesus when he apostrophized the hypocritical Scribes and Pharisees, saying, "Ye are the children of them who killed the prophets. Fill up then the measure of your fathers. Serpents, generation of vipers, how can ye escape from the judgment of Hinnom's Vale—απο της κρισεως της γεεννης, *apo tēs kriseōs tēs geennēs*?"[1] Many of those who very properly reject the notion of the book of Daniel revealing nothing beyond the reign of Antiochus Epiphanes, as erroneously imagine that "the prince" was Titus the Roman general, whose troops destroyed the holy, and took away the daily, and cast down the truth, Mosaically typified, to the ground. But Titus was certainly not the prince. He was *Sar* of the Gentile forces, not a *nahgid*; and no reason exists why this word should be applied to any other person than the Anointed Prince Royal referred to in the context. This was the prince, and the Romans were his people in the same sense in which Nebuchadnezzar and the Chaldees were God's. When Jehovah send Nebuchadnezzar and his forces against Judah and other nations to destroy them for their wickedness, they were the sword of the Lord. Speaking of this conqueror, he styles him, "Nebuchadnezzar the king of Babylon, my servant;" and in overthrowing Tyre, Jehovah says, "The

---

(1) Mat. xxiii. 29–33.

Chaldeans *wrought for me;*" and in their operations against Egypt, he says, "I will strengthen the arms of the king of Babylon, and put my sword in his hands." It was so with the Romans, although they knew it not. They wrought for the Prince Royal of Israel against rebellious Judah, who refused to acknowledge him as their king. See the parable comparing the kingdom of the heavens to a certain king who makes a marriage for his son. After he is raised from the dead, messengers are sent to invite Judah to the marriage; but they took his servants and slew them. "But when the king heard thereof he was wroth; and he sent forth *his* armies, and destroyed those murderers, and *burned their city."* [1] What armies were these Jesus styles *the king's armies?* There is but one answer that can be given—they were the Royal Father's, and therefore also the Prince Royal, his Son's; or in the words of the man Gabriel, "the people of the Prince." This explains the meaning of "an army being given to the Little Horn of the Goat against the evening-morning sacrifice." The Prince put them in commission for that work; and no doubt, though invisible, superintended the operations of the siege. Hence the coming of the Roman eagles against Judah's carcase,[2] as Moses had predicted,[3] was also *the coming,*[4] though not *the appearing,* of the Son of Man. If the prince had not given the army against the city, the Roman eagles would have been stripped of all their feathers; and have met with a fate not less disastrous than that of the Assyrians of old.

The last place in which Messiah is mentioned in Daniel is where he is styled "Michael the great prince."[5] Here the word is *Sar,* not *nahgid,* as might be expected; seeing that the passage speaks of the time when the Russianized Latino-Greek confederacy is to be broken on the mountains of Israel by Judah's king. The phrase would have been better rendered *"Michael the great Commander,"* whose name well expresses his omnipotence, signifying *"Who like to God."* Because Gabriel in the tenth of Daniel speaks of a contemporary angel whom he calls Michael, some there are who think that Michael the great commander is he. But the identity of name is no proof that the same person is referred to in both places. Michael who aided Gabriel against the Angel-Prince of the kingdom of Persia was no doubt the angel-*sar* Jehovah appointed over Israel in the days of Moses, concerning whom he said, "Beware of him, and obey his voice; for my name (or divine power) is in him."[6] But in the time of trouble this angel is superseded by Jesus, who is the great power of God, and therefore styled "Michael the great commander."

15. WHAT SHALL BEFALL JUDAH IN THE LATTER DAYS.

The things recorded in the eight and ninth chapters gave Daniel more particularly to understand what should befall Judah and Jerusalem in "*the last days*" of the Mosaic constitution of things. The idea of a great national overthrow after the expiration of the Seventy Heptades, or 490 years, was distinctly impressed on his mind. But, then there was a long lapse of time to be accounted for in the history of Judah, *first* from the appearance of the Four Horns of the Goat in the place of the great horn that was broken until the occupation of Judea by the Little Horn that was to arise out of the Northern Horn of the Four: and *secondly,* from the destruction of the Holy City and suppression of the Daily unto the breaking of the Little Horn of the Goat without help to save it, and consequent deliverance of Judah by their great commander and prince in "*the latter days*" of the seven times of the kingdom of men. This was a דבר *dahvahr,* subject Daniel desired much to hear discoursed upon. His anxiety to understand had at length become so acute, that he mourned for its gratification during three whole weeks.

(1) Mat. xxii. 7.   (2) Deut. xxviii. 26.   (3) Mat. xxiv. 27, 28.   Deut. xxix. 49, 50.
(4) Mat. x. 23.   (5) Dan. xii. 1.   (6) Ex. xxiii. 20, 21.

At the end of that period, while near the Tigris, a man appeared to him whose appearance was representative of the Prince Royal in his glory. Compare Daniel's description of him in chapter x. 6 with John's in Rev. i. 13. Having recovered from the effects of "this great sight," the glorious-looking personage informed him that he was sent to him to answer to his desire; and that his mission was to make him understand *what should befall his people in the latter days;* because the vision was *still for days;* that is, beyond the 490 years of the Seventy Heptades: and that he would show him what was noted in the scripture of truth. The eleventh and twelfth chapters contain the revelator's discourse, which Daniel says he understood.

In the beginning of the tenth chapter he informs us that "*the time appointed was long.*" When the truth of the matter was revealed to Daniel, the third year of Cyrus had arrived, B. C. 535. The first event of the vision he had witnessed; that, namely, of the Persian Horn of the Ram exceeding the Median Horn in altitude. This was 81 years before the commencement of the 2300 evening-morning, which terminated some ten or a dozen years ago. The vision, however, is still for days, which will not expire until the Seven Times of the kingdom of Babylon shall have ended in the reconcentration of the power of the עם־קדש *am-kôdesh*, or Holy People. Then all things foretold in the Book of Daniel will be finished.[1] Well might it be said, "the time appointed is long." Upwards of 2390 years have elapsed since the first year of Cyrus' sole reign, or the third after his conquest of Babylon, when "the word was revealed unto Daniel;" and, as it will be shown, fifty-six more will be required for the full accomplishment of the things which are noted in the Scriptures of truth.

The word revealed, then, may be distributed into three sections: the *first* terminates at the end of the thirty-fifth verse of the eleventh chapter; the *second* ends at the conclusion of the thirty-ninth; and to the *third* belongs the rest of the chapter to the end of the twelfth.

From the third verse the discourse treats of the Goat's notable horn in respect of the succession to his dominion; and from the fifth to the twenty-ninth, of the mutual rivalries, wars, and policy of the northern and southern horns of the Goat; and from the thirtieth to the thirty-third inclusive, of the indignation of the northern horn against Judah, Jerusalem, and the evening-morning sacrifice; and the thirty-fourth and thirty-fifth verses, of the help the Jews experienced under the Asmoneans till they were subjected to the Little Horn of the Goat, or "nation of a fierce countenance, whose tongue they did not understand."

The *second section* is descriptive of the Latino-Greek Babylonian power which established its dominion over the territories of the northern and southern horns of the Goat, and over the Holy Land; and which was to prosper, or maintain its position to the exclusion of Judah till the indignation against them should be accomplished, or for a short space after the termination of the 2300 years.

The *third section* of the discourse reveals the reäppearance of the southern and northern horns of the Goat upon their ancient territories, and their reäction upon the Moslemized Latino-Greek Little Horn; the subjection of this form of it and the southern horn, to the northern horn; the invasion of the Holy Land by this Horn; the destruction of this power by Michael the great commander; the deliverance of Judah; the resurrection of some of the dead; and the reconcentration of the power of all the tribes of Israel, in a time of trouble such as the world has never known since the confusion of human speech.

If we may judge from the utter failures of commentators to interpret the eleventh of Daniel, it may be pronounced to be the most difficult and incomprehensible chapter in the Bible. Moses Stuart, formerly "Professor of Sacred Literature in

---

(1) Dan. xii. 7.

the Theological Seminary at Andover," tells us, that, at verse 20, "we come upon Antiochus Epiphanes, whose history (as we may almost name it) occupies the rest of the chapter!!!" This absurdity is but a specimen of the rest. In his "Commentary," he says, he follows "the simple grammatical interpretation;" hence, having assumed that the last verse of the eleventh refers to Antiochus's death, he makes the first verse of the twelfth announce the standing up of Michael to be at that time! This shows how little the grammatical interpretation is to be depended on apart from an understanding of the gospel of the Kingdom of God. Seeing then that these mere grammarians are ignorant of this gospel, it is no use wasting precious time in considering their speculations, which can never come out right, inasmuch as the gospel is no constituent of the materials from which they work out their conclusions. We shall be better employed in excavating the truth for ourselves. Let us, then, apply ourselves to the agreeable task, and see in what our labor will result.

In presenting the reader with an interpretation of this chapter I shall have regard to the above divisions of the revelator's discourse. I shall give it in the form of paraphrase, incorporating the prophecy with the interpretation, but at the same time giving the angel's words in *italics* to distinguish them from my own. I may remark as to the date, that the revelator introduces his discourse with an allusion to "the first year of Darius the Mede." This was also the first year of Cyrus, who reigned conjointly with Darius; so that the third year of Cyrus was the first of his reign by himself. The reigns of Darius and Cyrus will therefore count as one, after which four are to be reckoned.

16. PARAPHRASE OF THE ELEVENTH OF DANIEL
TO THE THIRTY-FIFTH VERSE INCLUSIVE.

Behold, there shall stand up yet three kings in Persia, namely, Ahasuerus, Smerdis, and Darius; *and the fourth*, or Xerxes, *shall be far richer than they all: and by his strength through his riches he shall stir up all against the realm of Grecia. And* Alexander the Macedonian, *a mighty King, shall stand up, ruling with great dominion and doing according to his will. And when he shall stand up*, having suffered no defeat, *his kingdom shall be broken, and shall be divided* into four horns or kingdoms *toward the four winds of heaven: and* their glory and power shall fall *not to his posterity, nor according to* the extent of *his dominion which he ruled: for his kingdom shall be plucked up, even for other* rulers *besides those* of his family. *And the King of the South shall be strong, and shall be one of his*, Alexander the Great's, *princes* or generals; *and he shall be strong above him, and have dominion; his dominion shall be a great dominion*, extending over Egypt, Libya, Cyrenaica, Arabia, Palestine, Cœle-Syria, and most of the maritime provinces of Asia Minor, with the Island of Cyprus, and several others in the Ægean Sea, and even some cities of Greece, as Cicyon and Corinth. Such was the dominion of Ptolemy Soter, the first Macedonian King of Egypt.

VERSE 6. *And in the end of 52 years* from B. C. 301, *they*, the Kings of Egypt, and of the Assyro-Macedonian Horn of the north, *shall associate themselves together; for* Berenice, *the king's daughter of the south, shall come*, or be conducted, *to* Antiochus Theos, *the king of the north, to make a* marriage agreement; *but she shall not retain the power of the arm* of her father Ptolemy Philadelphus. *Neither shall he* her husband Antiochus *stand;* for Laodice his repudiated wife, whom he shall receive again when he divorces Berenice after her father's death, shall cause him to be poisoned. *Nor shall his arm*, Berenice, *stand; but she shall be given up* to suffer death; *and they*, the Egyptians also, *that brought her* to Syria; *and he*, her son, *whom she brought forth, and he that strengthened her in these times*, shall die; and thus leave her to the mercy of Laodice, which will be treachery and death.

VERSE 7. *But out of a branch of her* parent *roots shall* Ptolemy Euergetes her brother, *stand up in his estate* or kingdom, *and come with an army, and shall enter into* Antioch the capital, *and the fortress of the King of the north, and shall deal,* or make war, *against them,* even against Laodice and her son Seleucus, *and shall prevail: and* Euergetes *shall also carry captives into Egypt their gods, with their princes, and with their precious vessels of silver and gold: and he shall continue to* reign nine *more years than the King of the north,* who shall die a prisoner in Parthia five years before the King of Egypt. *So the king of the south shall come into his kingdom, and shall return into his own land,* B. C. 244.

VERSE 10. *But his* Seleucus' Callinicus' *sons,* Seleucus Ceraunus and Antiochus, *shall be stirred up* to war; *and shall assemble a multitude of great forces: and one of them,* even Antiochus the Great, *shall certainly come and overflow* through the passes of Libanus, *and pass through* into Galilee, and possess himself of all that part of the country which was formerly the inheritance of the tribes Reuben and Gad, and of the half tribe of Manasseh. *Then,* the season being too far advanced to prolong the campaign, *shall he return* to Ptolemais, where he shall put his forces into winter-quarters. *But* early in the spring, B. C. 217, Ptolemy Philopater shall march with a large army to Raphia, by which Antiochus *shall be stirred up* again to war, and defeated with great slaughter, so that he shall retreat *to his fortress.* Thus *shall the king of the south be moved with choler, and come forth, and fight with the king of the north ;* and the King of the north *shall set forth a great multitude,* even 72,000 foot and 6,000 horse; *but the multitude shall be given into the hand* of the King of Egypt.

And when he, the King of the south, *had taken away the multitude* by a signal defeat of Antiochus, *his heart shall be lifted up,* for he will desire to enter the Most Holy Place of the temple. But while he was preparing to enter, he was stricken and carried off for dead. In his victory over Antiochus, *he shall cast down ten thousands,* even 10,000 foot and 300 horse. *But* not following up his advantages, Philopater *shall not be strengthened* by his victory. *For* Antiochus *the king of the north shall return and shall set forth a multitude* of troops *greater than the former, and shall certainly come after certain,* that is, nineteen *years* after the battle of Raphia, or B. C. 198, *with a great army and with much riches,* and shall subjugate all the Holy and Cœle-Syria.

VERSE 14. *And in those times,* when Ptolemy Epiphanes shall reign over Egypt, *many shall stand up against the* infant *king of the south,* even the kings of Macedonia, and of Syria, and Scopas, the general of his deceased father. *But the Deputies of the Breakers of thy people,* Judah, O Daniel, that is, of the Romans, *shall interfere to establish the vision.* The Romans became the guardians and protectors of Epiphanes during his minority. They appointed three deputies, who were ordered to acquaint the Kings with their resolution, and to enjoin them not to infest the dominions of their royal pupil; for that otherwise they should be forced to declare war against them. The deputy Emilius, one of the three, after delivering the message of the Roman Senate, proceeded to Alexandria, and settled every thing to as much advantage as the state of affairs in Egypt would then admit. In this way the Romans began to mix themselves up with the affairs of Egypt, Syria, and the Holy; and in a few years established themselves as lords paramount of the East, being thus constituted a Power in Asia, which is symbolized in this relation by the Little Horn on the Northern Horn of the Grecian Goat; and in the 36th verse of this chapter, styled "THE KING." *But,* though destined to be *"* the Breakers of Judah," the assurance was given to Daniel, saying, *they shall fall.*

So the king of the north, being checked by the Roman Deputies, *shall come* into the Holy, *and cast up a mount* against Sidon, where he shall besiege the forces of the Egyptians; *and he shall take* Jerusalem, *the city of munitions,* from the castle of which he shall expel the Egyptian garrison; *and the arms of the south shall not withstand, neither his chosen people, neither shall there be any strength to withstand* Antiochus. *But* Antiochus *who cometh against* Ptolemy Epiphanes *shall do according to his own will* in Cœle-Syria and the Holy Land, *and none shall stand before him: and he shall* make a permanent *stand in the land of the glory which by his hand shall be consumed. He shall also set his face to enter* into Greece *with the strength of his whole kingdom, and Israelites with him. Thus shall he do* to incorporate Greece with his dominion, by which the Romans who had recently proclaimed it free, would be stirred up against him. Therefore, to secure the neutrality of their Egyptian ally, *he shall give* Cleopatra, *the daughter of women*, or princess royal, to Epiphanes to wife, *corrupting her* to betray him by resigning to him Cœle-Syria and Palestine as her dower, but on condition that he should receive half the revenue. Thus the land of Judah was given over as a bribe to bind Cleopatra to her father's interests, that she might influence Epiphanes either to remain neutral, or to declare against the Romans, his protectors. But *she shall* cleave to her husband, and *not stand, neither be for him*, but shall join with her husband in congratulating the Roman Senate on the victory they had gained over her father at Thermopylæ.

After this shall Antiochus, at the earnest solicitation of the Ætolians, *turn his face unto the isles* of Greece, *and shall take many: but a chieftain*, (kotzin,) L Scipio, the Roman Consul, *shall cause the reproach offered by him to cease; without his own disgrace he*, Scipio, *shall cause it to turn upon* Antiochus, by defeating him at Mount Sipyllus, and repulsing him from every part of Asia Minor. As the condition of peace, the Romans required him to pay 15,000 talents—500 down, 2500 on the ratification of the treaty, and the rest in twelve years at 1000 talents per annum. These terms being acceded to, *he shall turn his face toward the fortress*, or capitol, *of his own land*, being much at a loss how to raise the tribute. While in the province of Elymais, he heard of a considerable treasure in the temple of Jupiter Belus. He accordingly broke into it in the dead of night, and carried off all its riches. *But he shall stumble, and fall, and not be found;* for the provincials, exasperated at the robbery, rebelled against him, and murdered him and all his attendants, B. C. 187.

VERSE 20. *Then shall stand up in* Antiochus' *estate* or kingdom, his son Seleucus Philopater, *one who causeth an exactor to pass over the glory of the kingdom;* the business of his reign being to raise the tribute for the Romans. *But within few days*, that is twelve years, *he shall be destroyed, neither in anger nor in battle*, being poisoned by Heliodorus, his prime minister, having reigned long enough to pay the last instalment to the Romans.

VERSE 21. *And in his*, Seleucus Philopater's, *place shall stand up* Heliodorus, *a vile person*, being both a poisoner and usurper, *to whom they*, the authorities of the nation, *shall not give the honor of the kingdom: but* Antiochus Epiphanes *shall come in peaceably, and obtain the kingdom by flatteries* bestowed on the adherents of Heliodorus.

VERSE 22. *And with the arms of a flood*, by which they shall be formidably invaded, *shall they*, the Egyptians, *be overflown* from *before* Antiochus, whom they excite to war, by demanding the restitution of Cœle-Syria and Palestine. *And they shall be broken*, or subdued; yea, also, Onias, the High Priest, *or Prince of the* Mosaic Covenant, shall be murdered, as it came to pass B. C. 172. *And after the league made with* Ptolemy Philometer, Antiochus *shall work deceitfully* after his second invasion of Egypt, B. C. 170; *for he shall come up* to Alexandria, *and he shall become strong with a small people*, or army. By his deceit, *he shall enter peaceably even upon the fattest places of the province* to which he reduces Egypt; *and he*, Antiochus, *shall do that which his fathers*, or predecessors on the throne, *have not done*, nor his fathers' fathers; namely, *he shall scatter among* his followers *the prey, and spoils, and riches:* yea, *he shall forecast his devices against the strongholds* of Egypt, *even for a time. And he shall stir up his power and his courage against the king of the south with a great army; and the king of the south shall be stirred up to battle with a very great and mighty army; but he shall not stand:* for the Alexandrians seeing him in the hands of Antiochus, and lost to them, *shall forecast devices against him*, and place the crown of Egypt on the head of his brother, Euergetes II. *Yea, they that feed of the portion of Philometer's meat, even his courtiers, shall separate*, or renounce, *him; and his* Antiochus' *army shall overflow* Egypt; *and many* of the Egyptians *shall fall down slain. And the hearts of both these kings shall be to do mischief, and they shall speak lies at one table, but shall not prosper; for the end is still at the time appointed.*

Then shall Antiochus return into his land with great riches; and his heart shall be against the Covenant of the Holy; and he shall do terrible things against Jerusalem, taking it by storm, butchering 80,000 men, making 40,000 prisoners, and causing a like number to be sold for slaves. *And then shall he return to his own land*, laden with the spoils of the Temple, amounting to 1800 talents, or £270,000, about $1,315,000.

At the time appointed, under pretence of restoring Philometer to the throne, *he shall return and come towards the south*, against Alexandria to besiege it. *But it, this fourth invasion, shall not be as the former, or as the latter.* He raised the siege and marched towards Memphis, where he installed Philometer as king. As soon, however, as he had departed, Philometer came to an understanding with Euergetes, and they agreed to a joint reign over Egypt. This coming to the ears of Antiochus, he led a powerful army against Memphis, for the purpose of subduing the country. Having nearly accomplished his project, he marched against Alexandria, which was the only obstacle to his becoming absolute master of Egypt. But the Roman Embassy, sent at the request of the Ptolemies, met him about a mile from the city. They had left Rome with the utmost diligence. When they arrived at Delos they found a fleet of Macedonian, or Greek, ships, on board of which they embarked for Alexandria, where they arrived at the crisis of his approach: Popilius delivered to Antiochus the decree of the Senate, and demanded an immediate answer. Sorely against his will he agreed to obey its mandate, and draw off his army from Egypt. Thus, his invasion terminated very differently from the former and the latter; *for the ships of Chittim shall come against him*, and prevent him from incorporating Egypt into his Assyrian dominion of the north. Thus, the prophecy of Balaam, that "ships from the coast of Chittim shall come and afflict Asshur," began to show itself; a more complete fulfilment remains for the latter days, when "Asshur shall perish for ever."

All Antiochus' wrath was kindled at this interference; *therefore he shall be grieved, and return, and have indignation against the Covenant of the Holy;* for in his return-march, through Palestine, he detached 20,000 men under Apollonius with orders to destroy Jerusalem, B. C. 168. *So shall he do; he shall even return and have intelligence with them that forsake the Covenant of the Holy.*

VERSE 31. *And arms shall stand on his part* under Apollonius; *and they*, the Assyro-Macedonian troops, *shall penetrate the temple*, הַמִּקְדָּשׁ, ham-mikdosh, *the stronghold, and they shall remove the Daily, and they shall place* a statue of the Olympian Jupiter in the temple, and a strong garrison in the castle to command it, as *the abomination making desolate* its courts, and overawing the nation.

As soon as Antiochus Epiphanes was returned to Antioch, he published a decree by which all his subjects were required to conform to the religion of the State. This was aimed chiefly at the Jews, whose religion and nation he was resolved to extirpate. Atheneus, a man advanced in years, and extremely well versed in all the ceremonies of Grecian idolatry, was commissioned to carry the edict into effect in Judea and Samaria. As soon as he arrived at Jerusalem he began by suppressing *the Daily*, or evening-morning sacrifice, and all the observances of the Mosaic Law. He caused the sabbaths and other festivals to be profaned;

forbade the circumcision of children; carried off and burned all copies of the Law and the Prophets wherever they could be found; and put to death whoever acted contrary to the decree of the king. To establish it the sooner in every part of the nation, altars and chapels filled with idols were erected in every city, and sacred groves were planted. Officers were appointed over these, who caused the people generally to offer sacrifice in them every month, on the day of the month on which the king was born, who made them eat swine's flesh and other unclean animals sacrificed there. The temple in Jerusalem was dedicated to Jupiter Olympius, whose statue was placed in it. Thus he did in his great indignation against the Covenant of the Holy Nation and its Land.

VERSE 32. *And such of the Jews as do wickedly against the covenant shall Antiochus, by flatteries, cause to dissemble.* These not only "forsook the covenant of the holy," but "had intelligence" with the king, and aided him all they could in the desolation with which he was overspreading their country. *But the Maccabees and their adherents, people who do know their God, shall be strong, and do valiantly in war. And they,* even Mattathias and his five sons, and others with them, *that understand among the people, shall instruct* and encourage *many; yet they,* of the Maccabean party, *shall fall by the sword, and by flame, by captivity, and by spoil,* evils incident to the war, for *days,* that is, seven years from the ninth of Antiochus, the Era of the Asmoneans, to the third of Demetrius Soter, B. C. 161.

Now, when they shall fall by these seven years' calamities, *they shall be holpen with a little help;* for while Antiochus was amusing himself in celebrating games at Daphne, Judas Maccabæus had raised the standard of independence, and was helping his countrymen in Judea. He levied a small army, fortified the cities, rebuilt the fortresses, threw strong garrisons into them, and thereby awed the whole country. He defeated and killed Apollonius, and made great slaughter of the troops. With 3000 men he defeated Lysias with 47,000; and another army of 20,000 under Timotheus and Bacchides; and in the year before Christ 170, he gave Lysias a second defeat at Bethsura, by which he dispersed 65,000 of the enemy. The "*little help*" they received at this crisis was mingled with the supernatural, which will account for the extraordinary victories of the Jews over such powerful armies of Greeks with such unequal forces. In the battle with Timotheus near Jerusalem, it is related, that "When it waxed strong there appeared in sight of the enemy, from heaven, five comely men upon horses with bridles of gold, and two of them led the Jews, and took Maccabæus betwixt them, and covered him on every side with their weapons, and kept him safe, but shot arrows and lightnings against the enemies; so that being confounded with blindness, and full of trouble, they were killed."[1] Also, in the battle against Lysias, near Bethsura, with his 80,000 Greeks, Maccabæus and the Jews prayed that Jehovah would send a good angel to deliver Israel. In answer to this, as they were marching from Jerusalem, "there appeared before them, on horseback, one in white clothing, shaking his armor of gold. Thus they marched forward in their armor, ready not only to fight with men, but with most cruel beasts, and to pierce through walls of iron, having *an helper from heaven:* for Jehovah was merciful to them. And giving a charge upon their enemies like lions, they slew 11,000 footmen, and 1,600 horsemen, and put all the other to flight."[2] Thus were "they holpen with a little help" from heaven, and their struggle for independence crowned with success. Yet, in that struggle *many* did *cleave to them with flatteries:* trial was, therefore, necessary that the approved might be manifested to God. Hence, it was determined that *the party of the wise shall be weak, to try them, and to purify, and make them white* FOR THE TIME OF THE END; for then their services will be needed to assist in overthrowing the Kingdom of Babylon, and in taking the kingdom under the whole

---

(1) 2 Mac. x. 29.   (2) 2 Mac. xi. 8.

heaven, as shown to Daniel in the first year of Belshatzar. The Era of the Asmoneans was not that end; for, having particularized the events of the era, the revelator added, it is *still for a time appointed.*

We have now arrived at the end of the thirty-fifth verse, the events of which bring us down to the conclusion of 430 years from the destruction of the city and temple in the 19th of Nebuchadnezzar. There is here a change of topic in the prophecy. No more is said about Judah's warfare with the Greek Powers of the north or south. History, but not the prophecy, informs us that Judah became a kingdom, under princes of the Asmonean family, until it passed under the sceptre of Herod the Idumean, in the 37th year of whose reign JESUS CHRIST was " born KING OF THE JEWS." Not long after this event " *the sceptre departed from Judah,*" to whom it has never returned as yet, though earnestly desired and expected by all who believe the gospel of the Kingdom of God. When 28 years and 3 months old, the things revealed by Gabriel,[1] in relation to the seventieth heptade, began to be accomplished. During that seven years Judah's heart was stirred up from its lowest depths. John the Baptist and Jesus, the greatest personages of the time, turned all minds to that great kingdom, which, in the hands of the Prince Royal and the Saints, is to rule over all. But even then, " the end was still for a time appointed." Nearly 1830 years have passed since the expiration of the seventieth heptade. Judah has been broken, but their " *breakers*" have not been "*ground to powder*" by the Stone. The time, however, fast approaches; and the nearer it arrives, the more important do all questions become bearing upon Judah's land, and Zion, the city of their king.

About 95 years after the end of the 430 years previously indicated, the Asiatic kingdom of the north, which had so terribly afflicted Judah, was annexed by Pompey to the empire of the Romans, which, by the absorption of Greece, had now become Romano, or Latino-Greek; and in about thirty-five years after that, Egypt experienced the same fate. The kingdom of the Jews still survived. Two powers alone existed. The Four Horns of the Goat had disappeared; and nothing of the symbol remained but that which answered to the Romano-Greek Asiatic Power, waxing exceeding great toward the east, and looking with a fierce and threatening countenance upon the little kingdom of Judea. What shall this power be called? Gabriel styled it " *a Little Horn*" budding forth out of one of the four horns of the Goat—"*little*" in its Asiatic beginning, but "*exceeding great*" when it had ceased to grow. In relation to the Holy Land it appeared as a power, first in the north. History therefore shows, that the horn of the north was the one of the four upon which Daniel beheld it. But it did not content itself with merely looking fiercely at Judah. It fought against Judea and conquered; and so firmly had it established itself in the Holy, that when Jesus was arraigned before it, Judah clamored for his death, crying, " We have no king but Cæsar!"

From the annexation of the Holy Land to the Roman empire by Pompey until the present time, it has been mainly subject to Rome and Constantinople— to Rome until the throne of the empire was transferred by Constantine the Great to the city called by his name. Because, therefore, the Holy Land and city have been in the main possessed by the Romano-Constantinopolitan *power;* and because that power crucified the King of the Jews, and destroyed the holy soon after the seventieth heptade; and because it is the same (though administered by a different race and generation, that is, the Moslem) that will stand up against heaven's Commander in Chief in the approaching " consummation"—the power is represented by one and the same symbol, which is styled " the Little Horn" of the Grecian Goat, or nation.

But before dismissing the interpretation of the first section of the revelator's discourse, I would add some further remarks concerning the

(1) Dan. ix. 24, 27.

17. END OF THE MACCABEAN HEPTADE.

This epoch is particularly interesting as the end of Ezekiel's 430 years.[1] The house of Israel and the house of Judah had been great transgressors of the Covenant of the Holy, from the foundation of the temple, in the fourth year of Solomon, to the sack of the city and temple in the 19th of Nebuchadnezzar.[2] This was a period of 430 years, which was divided into two unequal periods; namely, one of *forty years*, from the foundation of the temple to the apostasy of Rehoboam and Judah; the other of *three hundred and ninety* from this apostasy to the destruction of the temple. The God of Israel determined that this long national trangression should be punished by as long a retribution. He, therefore, gave Israel "*a sign*" of what was coming upon them. This sign consisted in Ezekiel's lying on his left side 390 days, and then upon his right for 40 days more. By this was represented the prostrate condition of Judah and his companions from the other tribes, for 430 years. The 430 years of transgression had not quite ended when the sign was appointed, in the fifth of Jehoiachin's captivity. The thing signified began to take effect in the sacking of Jerusalem. Judah then began to "eat their defiled bread among the Gentiles;" so that the 430 years would end B. C. 160. These four centuries of punishment were a very calamitous period of Judah's history. They endured a captivity in Babylon for 70 years; for several years longer their times were "troublous;" they were vassals to the Ram dynasty of the kingdom of Babylon till it was superseded by Alexander the Great, the Notable Horn of the Macedonian Goat: afterwards, as we have seen, they were alternately subject to the Greek kings of Egypt and Assyria, and "the holy" became a field of battle for the hosts of these contending powers, who defiled the temple, and finally converted it into a house for the worship of the Olympian Jupiter. At length, and after all these terrible vicissitudes, and about *seven years* before the 430 years were about to expire, Judas Maccabeus, as the chieftain of a weak, but patriotic, intelligent, and devout, party of his countrymen, having a zeal for God and his holy law, commenced a war against Antiochus Epiphanes, illustrious for his zeal for Gentilism, his warlike propensities, and his cruel and bitter hatred of the Jews. The war ended in the deliverance of Jerusalem from his desolating abomination, the purification of the temple from the insignia of idolatry, its rededication to Jehovah, and the conversion of the Commonwealth into an independent kingdom, under the Levitical family of Asmoneus, in which the sovereignty continued for 129 years, till it was transfered to Herod the Idumean by the Romans, B. C. 37.

18. "THE KING," OR CONSTANTINOPOLITAN AUTOCRACY.

The second section of the revelator's discourse, which commences at the thirty-sixth verse and ends at the thirty-ninth inclusive, is a more amplified description of the Little Horn power than that previously given in the eighth chapter. The following is a corrected translation of the testimony:

"And out of one of them (one of the horns) came forth a Little Horn, which waxed exceeding great against the south, and against the east, and against the glory (of the land.) And it waxed great above the army of the heavens; and of the army and the stars it cast down to the ground, and stamped upon them. And against the Commander of the army it magnified, and by it the evening-morning sacrifice was taken away, and the foundation of its holy place scattered. And an army was given against the daily sacrifice because of rebellion, and it cast down the truth to the ground; and it wrought and prospered.[3]

And in the latter time of their kingdom, (the dominion of the four horns,) so as

---

(1) Ezek. iv. 1–8.   (2) Jer. lii. 12.   (3) Dan. viii. 9–12.

to cause the transgressors to fill up their measure, there shall stand up a king of fierce countenance, and understanding an intricate language. And his power shall be mighty, but not in his own virility; and he shall destroy wonderfully, and shall prosper and work; and shall destroy multitudes, and the people of the holy ones. And through his policy, also, he shall cause falsehood to prosper by his power; and because of his heart he shall do proudly, and in tranquillity he shall destroy many; he shall also stand up against the Commander of chieftains; but he shall be broken without help.[1]

"And the king shall work according to his pleasure, and he shall exalt himself and magnify himself against every mighty one, and he shall utter marvellous things concerning the Mightiest of the mighty, and he shall cause to prosper till the indignation be accomplished; for that that is determined shall be done. But to the gods of his predecessors he shall give no heed, nor to the delight of women, nor to any god shall he attend; for he shall become great above all.

"But he shall do honor to a god of guardians in his realm; even to a god whom his predecessors knew not, shall he do honor with gold and silver, and with costly gems and precious things. Thus shall he do to the Bazaars of the Guardians pertaining to a strange god, whom he shall acknowledge (and) exalt (with) riches; and shall cause them to rule over many; and he shall divide the land for a price."[2]

Here is a power which is to "prosper till the indignation" against Judah " be accomplished." The present condition of the Jews makes it evident to all that divine indignation against them still exists: hence the conclusion is necessary, that the Little Horn power is one of the powers that be.

The prophecy concerning "the King" in the eighth chapter is evidently descriptive of the Latino-Greek power in its pagan constitution, known in history as the destroyer of Jerusalem, and Judah "the people of the holy ones;" but with a hint also of its future ecclesiastical peculiarity, as appears from the testimony that "*through his policy he shall cause falsehood to prosper by his power.*" These few words are descriptive of the character, or nature of the power since Constantine the Great set up its throne in Constantinople to the present hour; and will be so preeminently, when its administration shall pass from the Sultan, to the Autocrat of All the Russias. As the head of a confederacy of the adherents of the Greek and Latin churches, it will be his policy to cause their priesthoods to be respected as useful coöperators in the subjection of Europe to his will.

This ecclesiastical policy of the Constantinopolitan Autocracy is enlarged upon in the description of it set forth in the eleventh chapter, where it is more particularly regarded in its catholic constitution without taking into the account the division of the Babylonian superstition into Greek and Latin catholic churches. Whatever may be the individual prejudices existing between individuals of the two schisms matters not; their ecclesiastics, whose spiritual authority is death-stricken by infidelity, on the principle of self-preservation, will have to place themselves under the shadow of the Autocrat, as Greeks and Latins have already done in the present dominions of the Czar.

In studying the nature of the Little Horn power it must not be regarded as a purely civil and military, or as an ecclesiastical power *per se*. It is both; but in describing it two classes of administrators are personified, the one as "*the king,*" and the other, as "*a god of guardians, whom his* (pagan) *predecessors knew not,*" and therefore "*a strange god.*" The power is said to give "no heed to the delight of women." But under its pagan constitution, the emperors who were *Pontifices Maximi,* or High Priests, as well as the civil and military chiefs of the state, and their subordinates in the priesthood, did give heed to the delight of women; that is it was their pleasure to marry: but when this pagan constitution of the power

---

(1) Dan. viii. 23-25.   (2) Dan. xi. 36–39.

was superseded by the Catholics as the consequence of the Constantinian revolution of the fourth century, the High Priesthood disappeared until its revival in the Bishop of Rome; so that he in Rome, and the emperor in Constantinople, became the representative incarnations of the civil and spiritual elements of the Latino-Greek Babylonian power. The imperial head still gave heed to "the delight of women," or, as some render it, "the desire of wives;" while the sacerdotal constituent of the power "forbids to marry, and commands to abstain from meats." [1]

Till the foundation of "*the Holy Roman*" dominion by Charlemagne and Leo, the bishop of Rome's imperial associate was the emperor at Constantinople; but when he could no longer afford him protection against the Longbeards he formed an alliance with the French emperor A. D. 800, which has politically obtained in the imperial line to this day. He is, however, at present in a peculiar and exceptional situation, which cannot become permanent. A pope and two emperors of the west is representative of two antagonist policies acting upon the same ecclesiastical centre which must result in collision, and terminate in the suppression of one of the emperors, that the normal constitution of things may be restored.

But the time is not far off, when the Latin Bishop will have to seek again to the Constantinopolitan Autocracy for protection. Daniel's prophecy of "the king" requires this; for he is to "cause to prosper till the indignation be accomplished." The pope and one of the emperors sustained by his power will place the Latino-Greek king "*above all*" the mighty, who shall be his contemporaries in "the time of the end."

But, for this manifestation to appear, the Ottoman dynasty must of course be driven out of Europe. The occupation of the Dragon's throne by a non-catholic royalty is clearly exceptional. The Ottoman has never, as a matter of fact, "magnified himself above all;" nor has he honored the Latin Bishop as a god in his dominion, or shown himself at all a gracious patron of his saints and their temples. The power causing falsehood, or False-Prophetism, to prosper, must hold Jerusalem at the crisis of the accomplishment of the indignation. By False-Prophetism, I mean, *papalism*. Hence, the Sultan must be ejected, that a dynasty patronizing a High Priest who forbids to marry, may come in. When, therefore, the Czar gets possession of Constantinople he will not be hostile to the pope. On the contrary, he will honor and acknowledge him, and exalt him; and be the enemy of the Holy Land.

As to the Ottoman, his existence in Constantinople is exceptional. His mission was to punish the Greek catholics, and the Latins also to some extent, for their excessive superstition and idolatry, with the loss of their sovereignty over "*a third part*" of the Latino-Greek Babylonian empire; and not to extinguish temporarily or finally the Little Horn power. As far as the Greeks were concerned, their sovereignty was abolished A. D. 1453. The Greek dynasty of the power gave place to the Turkish, while the horn itself remained. The destruction of the horn is reserved for Michael the great Commander of Judah, after it shall have come under the sovereignty of the king of the north. This existence of the Ottoman *régime* in the Kingdom of Babylon, may be regarded by way of illustration, as a splint upon a broken leg. It remains therefore the support of the limb until the fractured ends shall be reunited by *callus*, after which it is removed as useless. The brass and iron eastern limb of Nebuchadnezzar's Image received a fracture at the juncture of the two metals. The sovereignty of the kingdom of Babylon was no longer Greek and Latin; but, as at the present time, Latin and Ottoman. In "the time of the end," however, when the Image stands complete upon its Feet of Iron and Clay, sound constitutional limbs are indispensable. The time is now about

---

(1) 1 Tim. iv. 3.

come, when the Ottoman splint may be removed, and the Latino-Greek Leg of the Image repaired by Russian *callus* be permitted to stand under a *régime* more in consonance with the catholic constitution of the kingdom of Babylon. The unbinding of the splint is the present mission of "the Powers." It is obvious to all that the Turk is a useless excrescence upon society, occupying a position in the heaven of Churchdom for which he is not at all qualified by faith, civilization, or sympathy with contemporary despotisms. The Babylonians are all willing that he should be deposed from his sovereignty over the catholic populations; but they are not willing that the Byzantine empire should be revived under the Autocrat of All the Russias. Their antagonisms, however, for the prevention of this are the providential means to bring it about. Every step they take in the Eastern Question only makes this result more sure. The end, untoward enough for them, is decreed; and God has blinded them, ahitophelizing all their counsel, that it may come to pass.

The Little Horn of the Goat is brother to the Little Horn of the fourth beast with its Eyes and Mouth. Their fraternity is consequent upon the Latin element entering into the constitution of them both. Old Rome is the throne of the Little Horn with Eyes and Mouth; while New Rome, or Constantinople, is the throne of the Little Horn of the Goat. The former power is the New Roman Empire of the West founded by Charlemagne, which has never been as yet united to the Greek element of the kingdom of Babylon. It is styled "the Holy Roman" dominion, because their Holinesses the Popes are its High Priests. Hence, it is the *Latin* kingdom of heaven, beyond the pale of which, they say, there is no salvation! The Little Horn of the Goat represents the undivided power of the Kingdom of Babylon from the annexation of the northern kingdom to Rome, B. C. 65; to the loss of Italy, and the West; and of the same power *minus* Italy and the West from the eight century to the present time. But when the Autocrat gains Constantinople, and Russianizes Italy and the West; and having superseded the Ottoman *régime* in Asia, comes as Gog to invade the Holy Land and to besiege Jerusalem, the Little Horn of the Goat will again represent the power of the whole dominion briefly united under one chief, and he the proudest that ever exalted and magnified himself above all the rulers upon earth. In that near future the Little Horn of the Goat will be "exceeding great," comprehending all the sovereignties represented by the Two-Horned, and Ten-Horned, Beasts, and the Image of the Beast. But when it is "broken in pieces without help"—יד ישבר ובאפס *uvĕĕphes yahd yishsahvair*—it appears no more as a symbol upon the prophetic page. Its mission in the Holy Land and against Judah ends with its own Pharaoh-like destruction; and the East delivered, future events reōpen in the West, where only a Beast, the False Prophet, and the Ten Horns, their Russian Constantinopolitan confederacy being dissolved, remain to be ground to powder, and destroyed by fire and sword.

The "*policy*" of the Little Horn king in his Constantinian successorship to A. D. 1453 was, and will hereafter be, characterized by zeal for the baptized paganism known in history as the catholic religion. Justinian of all its crowned heads affords the most striking illustration of Daniel's description of it. His policy was truly ecclesiastical. "Never prince," says Dupin, "did meddle so much with what concerns the affairs of the Church, nor make so many constitutions and laws upon this subject. He was persuaded that it was the duty of an emperor, and for the good of the state, to have a particular care of the Church, to defend its faith, to regulate external discipline, and to employ the civil laws and the temporal power to preserve it in order and peace."

"Justinian," says Gibbon, "sympathized with his subjects in their superstitious reverence for living and departed saints; his Code, more especially his novels, confirm and enlarge the privileges of the clergy; and in every dispute between the monk and the layman, the partial judge was inclined to pronounce, that truth and innocence are always on the side of the Church. In his public and private devotions, he was assiduous and exemplary; his prayers, vigils, and fasts, displayed the austere penance of a monk; his fancy was amused by the hope, or belief, of personal inspiration; he had secured the patronage of the Virgin, and St. Michael, the archangel; and his recovery from a dangerous disease was ascribed to the miraculous succor of the holy martyrs, Cosmos and Damian. Among the titles of imperial greatness, the name of *Pious* was the most pleasing to his ear; to promote the temporal and spiritual interest of the Church was the serious business of his life; and the duty of father of his country was often sacrificed to that of *Defender of the Faith*. While the barbarians invaded the provinces, while the victorious legions marshalled under the banners of Belisarius and Narses, the successor of Trajan, unknown to the camp, was content to vanquish at the head of a synod."

Enmity to Judah and the disciples of Christ, whom it designates as heretics and schismatics, has been characteristic of the kingdom of Babylon under all its administrations. This feature of it is indicated in the saying, that "*In tranquillity he shall destroy many.*" The Constantinopolitan Little Horn as well as its imperial brother of the West, has abundantly vindicated its claim to this destructiveness. Justinian was no individual exception to this general character of the power. "His reign," says Gibbon, "was an uniform, yet various scene of persecution; and he appears to have surpassed his indolent predecessors both in the contrivance of his laws, and rigor of their execution. The insufficient term of three months was assigned for the conversion or exile of all heretics; and if he still connived at the precarious stay, they were deprived, under his iron yoke, not only of the benefits of society, but of the common birthright of men and Christians."

The high exaltation of the Constantinopolitan Autocracy in "the time of the end," previously to its standing up to "be broken without help" by Judah's Commander in Chief, is predicted in the words, "*He shall become great above all.*" Impious and cruel as Antiochus Epiphanes, and superstitious and fanatical as Justinian, with the arrogance, ambition, and profanity of the Latin Prophet in his palmiest days, this Sin-power administered by a Russian *régime*, will fully answer to all that has been predicated of Paul's "MAN OF SIN and *Son of Perdition*, who opposeth and exalteth himself above every one called a god, or an object of regard; so that in the temple of the god he sits as a god exhibiting himself because he is a god." The apostle then informs us of his destruction by Michael the great commander, saying, "That Lawless One shall the Lord consume with the Spirit of his mouth, (represented in the Apocalypse by a sword going out of his mouth,) and bring to an end with the manifestation of his presence: the coming of whom is according to the working of the adversary in all power, and signs, and lying wonders, and with all deceivableness of unrighteousness in them that perish."[1] This is not exclusively applicable to the Latin False Prophet; but to the power comprehensive of the civil, military, and spiritual elements as described by Daniel, and designated by Isaiah as "The King for whom Tophet is ordained of old."[2] When the sceptre falls from the feeble hands of the Sultan, the world will behold in his Muscovite successor a potentate unrivalled in presumption and impiety by any of his predecessors, not excepting Pharaoh of the olden time.

19. A GOD OF GUARDIANS, OR, THE LATIN PROPHET OF THE WEST.

"*To a god of guardians in his estate he shall do honor.*" The original is אֱלֹהַּ מָעֻזִּים *elōah mǎuzzim*, "a god of guardians:" and styled in the same connection, אֱלוֹהַּ נֵכָר *elōah naikhār*, "a strange god:"—a god appearing from among the Jew-

---

(1) 2 Thess. ii. 3, 4, 8, 9.   (2) Isai. xxx. 27–33; xxxi. 8, 9.

ish sect of the Nazarenes, and therefore a *foreign* god. *Eloah* is a passive participial noun, and applied to Christ in the phrase, משיח אלוה לִמֶנוּ *mashiach eloah limmenu,* "the Anointed One cursed for us;" that is, by the Law, which says: "Cursed is every one that hangeth upon a tree." The connection in which *eloah* is found determines whether it should be taken in a good or in a bad sense. In the passage before us it is used in any other than in a good sense. The god is therefore *an accursed one of guardians,* who is honored in the realm of the Little Horn of the Goat. From this it will be seen that Christ and Antichrist are both denominated "cursed," but on different grounds; Christ, because he became a curse for his people by hanging on a tree as an expiation for their sins; and Antichrist, he that sets himself up in Christ's place, and finally against him, because of his blasphemy against the Mightiest of all.

Mahuzzim is the plural of מעוֹז *mahōz, a fortress.* It is used *tropically* in Psalm lx. 9: "Ephraim is the *fortress* of my head," i. e. my helmet: and in Prov. x. 29, "a *fortress* to the upright is *the way of God,*" i. e. God's truth: *Protectors, defenders, guardians* are as fortresses to those who trust in them; hence the phrase, "Jehovah is my fortress," i. e., he is my guardian, &c.

But those who glory in the Eyes and Mouth of the Little Horn of the West, or in the God of Guardians, whom the Little Horn of the Goat delights to honor, (for the Eyes, Mouth, and god, are one and the same power,) seek for refuge in other fortresses than Jehovah. Chrysostom, in his homily on the martyrs of Egypt, says: "The bodies of those saints *fortify* the city more effectually for us than impregnable walls of adamant; and like towering rocks placed around on every side, repel not only the assaults of enemies that are visible, but the insidious stratagems also of invisible demons, and counteract and defeat every artifice of the devil as easily as a strong man overturns the toys of children." The Greeks and Latins made the most of these wonderful martyrs. Believing in ghosts, or disembodied human spirits, they proclaimed the translation of their shades to heaven to act as mediators and intercessors with the Virgin and her Son; but kept their bones and dust in church-shrines to protect, defend, or guard them from all enemies, demons, and other evils to which the flesh is subject. Speaking of these times of intense superstition, Gibbon says: "The Christians of the seventh century had relapsed into a semblance of paganism; their public and private vows were addressed to the relics and images that disgraced the temples of the East; the throne of the Almighty was darkened by a cloud of martyrs, saints, and angels, the objects of popular veneration; and the Collyridian heretics, who flourished in the fruitful soil of Arabia, invested the Virgin Mary with the name and honors of a goddess." It was to punish the East for these abominations, that the four prepared angels confining upon the Euphrates—the Seljuks, Zinghis Khan's Moguls, Tamerlane's hosts, and the Ottoman Turks—were loosed until they should come to be bound by the Danube, which defines the political geography appointed to exist between themselves and "the Rest of the Men (the Holy Roman Empire) which were not killed"—whose sovereignty was not overthrown—"by these plagues," inflicted by the four messenger, or angel, powers; "yet repented not of the works of their hands, that they should not worship demons (the imaginary ghosts of martyrs and saints) and idols of gold, and silver, and brass, and stone, and of wood; which neither can see, nor hear, nor walk: neither repented they of their murders, nor of their sorceries, nor of their fornication, (the especial vice of the priests who are forbidden to marry,) nor of their thefts."[1]

The bodies and ghosts of Romish saints and martyrs erected into guardian demons by "the church," were a cheap fortification for a city, temple, or country, requiring no rations; and if "the eloquent Chrysostom" be credited, a more

---

(1) Rev. ix. 14, 15, 20, 21.

impregnable defence than a whole host of embodied warriors armed to the very teeth! What chance, then, has the unlucky Turk who has no other *mahuzzim* than the Dardanelles and fortresses of like construction? St. Patrick of Ireland, St. George of England, St. Andrew of Scotland, and St. Denis of France, it may be inferred, are on his side at present; but whether these guardians will prove impregnable *fortresses* for "the common hereditary foe and tyrannical bloodhound, the Turk," as Czar Johann styled him in 1557, is very much to be doubted, seeing that his battle-cry is, "*Down with the Giaours*," which must be particularly offensive to the cloud of guardian demons on the other side.

The chief or prince of the ecclesiastical element of the Kingdom of Babylon is *god*, or chief pontiff of these *guardians*. He is in the Little Horn of the Goat's *estate*, which is coextensive with the territory of that dominion, when he stands up against the *Sar* of Israel. Justinian, whom I have indicated as the fittest representative of the civil element of the Power that has yet appeared in Constantinople in its dealings with the god, delighted to honor him. In a celebrated letter written by him to the Bishop of Rome, dated March, 533, and which thenceforth became part and parcel of the civil law, he is recognized, or "*acknowledged*," as the legal head of all the churches of the eastern and western provinces of the empire. "We suffer not," says the imperial writer, "any thing that belongs to the state of the churches to be done without submitting it to your holiness, *who art head of all the churches*." In this way, "the king who does according to his will," acknowledged this "strange god" as of supreme spiritual authority over all "the Bazaars of the Guardians," which became his.

To a god whom his predecessors knew not—to a strange god—shall he do honor. Previous to the reign of Constantine this "god of guardians" was unacknowledged by the emperors and constituted authorities of the Little Horn Power. They are therefore said not to have known him. There was then no Bishop of Rome, though there was a principal bishop of the anti-Novation or Catholic Church, called Christian, in Rome. Constantine made this chief of a corrupt majority chief magistrate of Rome for life, or Lord Mayor, in 313. His jurisdiction was confined to the city. But in 378, the emperor, who resided in Constantinople, extended his *spiritual* authority over all the churches of Italy and Gaul. His supremacy, however, was not limited to these. It continued to grow, until, in a hundred and fifty-five years after, Justinian could say to him, "*thou* ART *head of* ALL *the churches*," that is, of the Kingdom of Babylon. But while this was the fact, the Roman Bishop bore no title that indicated it. He shared with the bishops of Alexandria, Jerusalem, Antioch, and Constantinople, the honorary title of *Patriarch*, or Chief Father. These patriarchs had all equal power, and differed only in respect of rank and precedency; the Bishop of Rome being considered the first in rank, and this out of respect to the city in which he presided. A bishop of the name of Leo was the first that claimed jurisdiction over other churches on the ground of his being the successor of St. Peter; and when it was decreed at the Council of Chalcedon that the See of Constantinople should be *second to that of Rome* with respect to rank, assigning as a reason for it the preëminence of the city, this Patriarch was quite dissatisfied, because his preëminence was not founded on something more stable than the dignity of the city, and wished to have it rest on the authority of Peter as the founder of the See.[1] From this time this foundation for the preëminence of the See of Rome was urged with the greatest confidence; and though the ground on which it is assumed has slender claims to credibility, it does not appear to have been much disputed.

But the increasing pride, ambition, and vanity of the rising god were not long content to bear a title common to others whom he regarded as his inferiors in

---

(1) Sueur. A. D. 451.

every respect. He desired a title expressive of the universality of his acknowledged headship over ecclesiastical affairs in the Kingdom of Babylon. But the Patriarch of Constantinople, scarcely less arrogant and ambitious than himself, in a council held at that city in 588, assumed the title of *Universal Bishop*, which was confirmed to him by the council. This aroused the indignation of the contemporary bishop of Rome, with whom it was a principle to endure no ecclesiastical superior in the Little Horn dominion. He styled it, "an execrable, profane, and diabolical procedure." In 590, Gregory I, usually termed "the Great" by ecclesiastics, was the representative of the strange-god power. He wrote a letter to Maurice, who occupied the Dragon-throne, in which he styles the title "*a blasphemous name by which all honor is taken from all other priests, while it is foolishly arrogated by one.*" He says, it was offered to the Bishops of Rome by the Council of Chalcedon, but refused; "why," then says he, "should we refuse this title when it was offered, and another assume it without any offer at all?" He calls upon Maurice to humble and chastise the presumptuous patriarch, who, by taking upon himself the title, would elevate himself above the emperor. The letter, however, does not appear to have produced any effect; for the pompous title continued to be borne by the patriarchs of Constsantinople.

One of these whose name was Cynacus in a letter to Gregory subscribed himself "Universal Bishop." Gregory was greatly displeased, and in consequence treated the bearers of it uncourteously. These complained to the emperor, who wrote to Gregory, and advised him to be more friendly in future, and not to insist so far on *punctilios of style* as to create a scandal about a title, and to fall out about a few syllables. Gregory replied to this, that "the innovation in the style did not consist much in the quantity and alphabet; but the bulk of the iniquity was weighty enough to sink and destroy all. And therefore I am bold to say," says he, "that whoever adopts or affects the title of UNIVERSAL BISHOP has the pride and character of Antichrist, and is in some manner his forerunner in this haughty quality of elevating himself above the rest of his order. And indeed both the one and the other seem to split upon the same rock; for, *as pride makes Antichrist strain his pretension up to* GODHEAD, so whoever is ambitious to be called the only or Universal Prelate, arrogates to himself a distinguished superiority, and rises, as it were, upon the ruins of the rest."

Whether of the two should bear the title of Universal Bishop and transmit it to his successors, the Patriarch of Constantinople or the Patriarch of Rome, was the great politico-ecclesiastical question of the day. Had the dynasty of Maurice continued to occupy the Dragon-throne of the Little Horn, it is probable that the Bishop of Rome would have been excluded from the Babylonian Godship. But it was ordained otherwise. Phocas, a centurion, headed a rebellion of the troops against the emperor, whom he murdered with all his family, and then settled himself on the throne. This was A. D. 602. Gregory joyfully saluted the fortune of the assassin, celebrated the deliverance of the people, and the fall of Maurice, whom he styled, the oppressor. In 604, Gregory died, and was succeeded by Boniface III. who without scruple adopted the proud title in dispute. He had importunately begged it of Phocas, with the privilege also of transmitting it to all his successors. The profligate emperor, to gratify the inordinate ambition of this court sycophant, deprived the patriarch of Constantinople of the title he had hitherto borne, and conferred it upon Boniface, A. D. 606, at the same time declaring the Church of Rome to be the head of all other churches. He was very liberal to the bazaars of the guardians pertaining to the god, commonly called "churches," and allowed the Pantheon, a temple dedicated to *All the Gods* by his predecessors, to be turned into a bazaar or church devoted to *All the Saints*. Phocas was a diminutive, ill-favored monster in crime, and therefore the better qualified for a patron of the Roman bishop, who hailed him as the pious avenger of the church.

Two years after the promulgation of the decree, a pillar with a gilt statue on the top of it, was erected in Rome to the honor of Phocas with the following inscription—*Pro innumerabilibus Pietatis ejus beneficiis, et pro quiete procuratâ, ac conservatâ libertate.* Thus was memorialized the fulfilment of the sure word of prophecy, saying, "To a god of guardians in his estate, even to a god whom his predecessors knew not, a strange god, shall he acknowledge and exalt with riches." He strained up his pretensions to godhead, and as a god was recognized by the secular element of the Little Horn.

20. GUARDIANS' BAZAARS OR TEMPLES DEDICATED TO SAINTS.

"*To a god of guardians shall he do honor with gold, and silver, and with costly gems, and precious things. Thus shall he do to the Bazaars of the Guardians pertaining to the strange god.*"—The honor done to the Pontiff of the Mysteries of the worship of Guardian Saints by the emperor, was expressed not in mere decrees, but in the more substantial form of all kinds of riches. They were given to him in being bestowed upon the Bazaars dedicated to guardian saints, all of which throughout the empire were subordinated to him. Justinian's is a remarkable illustration of imperial liberality to the Roman god in the bestowal of riches upon his "churches," or bazaars of spiritual merchandise. Besides the magnificent temple of St. Sophia, which with 10,000 workmen he finished in five years, eleven months, and ten days from the first foundation, he dedicated twenty-five others in Constantinople and its suburbs to the honor of the Virgin and the saints of the catholic calendar. Most of these edifices were decorated with marble and gold. His munificence was diffused over the Holy Land; throughout which monasteries for both sexes were amply diffused. Almost every saint in the calendar acquired the honor of a bazaar; and the liberality with which he honored them was boundless. No wood except the doors was admitted into the construction of St. Sophia. Paul Silentiarius, who beheld its primitive lustre, enumerates the colors, the shades, and the spots of ten or twelve marbles, jaspers, and porphyries, which nature had profusely diversified, and which were blended and contrasted as it were by a skilful painter. "The triumph of Antichrist was adorned with the last spoils of paganism, but the greater part of these *costly stones* was extracted from the quarries of Asia Minor, the isles and continent of Greece, Egypt, Africa, and Gaul. A variety of ornaments and figures was curiously expressed in Mosaic; and the images of Christ, of the Virgin, of the Saints and of Angels, were exposed to the superstition of the Greeks. According to the sanctity of each object, *the precious metals* were distributed in thin leaves, or in solid masses. The spectator was dazzled by the glittering aspect of the cupola; the sanctuary contained forty thousand pounds weight of *silver;* and the holy vases and vestments of the altar were of the *purest gold*, enriched with *inestimable gems*." Such are the words of Gibbon—a literal, though inadvertent interpretation of the testimony with which this paragraph begins.

The Bazaars of the Guardians—מבצרי מעזים, *mivtzahrai mahuzzim.* The noun *mivtzahrai* is derived from the root בצר, *bahtzar*, which, among other meanings, signifies, *to enclose with a wall.* As a noun, בצר *bĕtzĕr* signifies ore of gold and silver, precious metals, store, or treasure so secured. Parkhurst has the following upon the word: "Derivative, *Bazaar*, a kind of covered market-place among the eastern nations, somewhat like our *Exeter 'Change* in London, but frequently much more extensive. Latin, or rather Punic, *Byrsa*, the *Burse* at Carthage;" equivalent to the French *Bourse*. In the English version the phrase is rendered, "*the most strong holds*," with which those who compiled the marginal references and readings were not satisfied; and therefore they have tried to improve it by the words "*fortresses of munitions.*" But if the reader can extract any sense out of these renderings it is more than I can. Moses Stuart renders it *fenced strong holds;* and the strange god he styles, "the god of strong holds, that is, the god who has power over them." He confesses, however, that verse 39 is "a difficult verse, which has occasioned many discrepant interpretations." He refers to Lengerke, who, he remarks, "makes the fenced strong holds to mean *temples,* and the sentiment to be, that the tyrant will do for temples and their foreign gods the same thing that v. 38 says he will do in respect to the *god of strong holds,* i. e. he will bestow many liberal presents upon them." As neither Lengerke nor Moses Stuart seem to see any thing in Daniel (the last chapter perhaps excepted) beyond the times of Antiochus, some hundred and sixty years, or so, before the birth of Jesus Christ, their *temples* and "strong holds" have relation to "fortified strong holds of foreigners" attacked by Antiochus, and temples of idols. Lengerke has almost fallen upon the correct meaning. Had he referred the *bětsar,* heëmantively written *mivtzahr,* to the temples of guardian saints instead of to those of the pagan Greeks, he would have hit the mark exactly: but then how could he be so uncharitable as to turn the pious father of Christendom into a strange god, and all the ecclesiastical buildings of that dominion dedicated to saints and angels, into Bazaars or places of traffic in spiritual merchandise and the bodies and souls of men!

The churches, chapels, and cathedrals, then, are the "most strong holds" of the superstition of the Kingdom of Babylon. They are the houses of business dedicated by the prospering craft to "guardian spirits." There are the images and pictures of the saints. They are Saints-Houses in which are deposited their shrines; silver, gold, and ivory crucifixes; old bones, and various kinds of votive trumpery. They are literally "dens of thieves," without ever having been the houses of the Father—dens, where people are robbed of their money under divers false pretences. They are places where pews are sold by auction, the proudest sittings being knocked down to Mammon's greatest favorites; places where fairs of vanity and deceit are held for "pious objects;" and where spiritual empirics pretend to "cure souls" in consideration of so much per annum. In view of these facts the scriptural epithet bestowed upon the church buildings of the Apostasy is most appropriate. They are truly Bazaars of spiritual merchandise; and *the prospering craft,* "the great men of the earth" made rich by trading in their wares, are the Bazaar-Men who extort all kinds of goods from their customers by putting them in fear, and comforting them with counterfeits upon some bank in the world to come. They buy and sell under license from the Ecclesiastical Power, having received its mark upon their foreheads, or on their right hands. The reader may find their catalogue of merchandise in the eighteenth of Revelation, twelfth and thirteenth verses. Among the articles received in exchange for spirituals are tithes, *bodies,*[1] and souls of men. But the trade of these soul-merchants is in any thing but a satisfactory state at present. Great numbers of their customers have discovered that the profit is all upon one side; nor are they backward in proclaiming that when a favorable opportunity presents they will break up the iniquitous concern, and make the cheats disgorge their unhallowed gains. This will be a sad day, a day of universal bankruptcy for the weeping and wailing merchants of Babylon; "for no man buyeth their merchandise any more." When a man's trade is thus extinguished, nothing but ruin stares the shattered tradesman in the face. This is the fate that awaits the preachers of all the gospels of the Bazaars— gospels other than Paul preached, and which leave men in ignorance and disobedi-

---

(1) How remarkably this is fulfilled in the trade carried on by "the ministers of religion" in dead bodies! They "consecrate" their bazaars, or a piece of ground for the burial of the dead. Having provided these "holy" receptacles, they persuade their followers that not to be buried there is to have the burial of a dog or a heathen. This causes the bodies of the dead to be brought to them for religious burial, which they perform for a sum of money expressed or understood.

ence; gospels which make them partisans of human crotchets and traditions; and the apologists of any thing sincerely professed as a substitute for the truth.

It is a remarkable feature in this prophecy that the Bazaars for priestly and clerical wares are distinguished from houses or shops of fair and honorable trade, by being styled *Bazaars of Mahuzzim*. When jewellers, bakers, hardwaremen, &c., open stores, they emblazon their 'signs with their own names; but when the clergy open houses for the exercise of their profession, they impose upon the ignorant public the idea that they belong to the apostles and their brethren! They say that these ancient worthies are still alive, and in heaven, and greatly interested in human affairs, especially in church-buildings and the things transacted there! Hence they put their statues in niches, and on parapets, and make them presents of the churches, as is clear from the names they bear; as, St. Sophia at Constantinople, St. Peter's at Rome, Our Lady's at Paris, St. Paul's at London, and so forth. The imposition, however, consists in this, that while they give these buildings to the "departed spirits" they call by these names, they will not permit the gospel the apostles preached, and the institutions they ordained, to be announced within their walls; but perversely persist in excluding it, and in making it of none effect by their vain and foolish traditions. But the whole system is a cheat, and a very profitable one for the present to those who live by it. It is ecclesiastical craft caused to prosper by the civil power; and it will prosper until Israel's Commander shall bring it to an end, and cause the truth by his energy to prevail at last.

Having illustrated somewhat in detail the terms of this remarkable prophecy, I proceed to remark that the Little Horn of the Goat and Daniel's Fourth Beast are both representative of "The King of Fierce Countenance" at the time when the Commander in Chief shall break the former in pieces; and the Saints shall take away the dominion of the latter, to consume and destroy it as the fiery flame and wheels of burning fire issuing forth from the Ancient of Days. The Goat's Little Horn and the god he honors, are equivalent to the Beast, the Little Horn with its Eyes and Mouth, and the Ten Horns, at *the time of the breaking of the Goat-Horn*. This identity of representation will not have been always so; for about the conclusion of the eighth century, the Goat-Horn and its god, only represented the Constantinopolitan Civil Power, whose jurisdiction had almost entirely ceased from Italy and the West; and the Roman Ecclesiastical, which, disappearing from the East, was recognized in the Popes by all the nations of the West, who, in the words of Gregory II. to the emperor, "revere as a god upon earth, the apostle St. Peter, whose image you threaten to destroy;" and therefore, also, so regarded "Christ's Vicegerent," who claimed to be Peter's successor in the godship. The Ten Horns with crowns, and the Eleventh Horn, of the Beast, have never yet been subject to the Goat-Horn; though the territory on which they exist as powers has before their existence: not all the territory of the Eleventh Horn, however, but so much of it as it possesses within the frontiers of the old Roman dominion.

But, though the Little Horn of the Goat, or Constantinopolitan Power, has never been Lord of the European Continental Powers represented by the Eleven Horns, the time is at hand when it will acquire that dominion. The feeble Ottoman must be ejected from the throne to make room for a more powerful and vigorous dynasty. This dynasty will be the last occupant of the throne of the Constantinopolitan Power for a thousand years. During its enthroned existence it will be all that is affirmed of the Little Horn of the Goat, and of "the King that does according to its will," in the eighth and eleventh chapters of Daniel. At this crisis, its power will be mighty, and it will destroy wonderfully, and prosper, and practise. As Lord of Europe and Asia the continental dynasties of the West will be gathered unto it. They will acknowledge its supremacy, and seek to it as the shadow and strength of their dominions. The Constantinopolitan Little Horn Power will then be in final fourth-beast manifestation, " dreadful, and terrible, and strong exceedingly; having great iron teeth; devouring and breaking in pieces, and *stamping the residue* WITH THE FEET *of it;* and having ten horns." It is while the post-Ottoman dynasty occupies the throne that the " stamping the residue with the feet of" the beast is accomplished. The Feet represent a power, a stamping or conquering power, which subjects "*the residue*" to its dominion. The claws of these feet are of *brass*, while the feet themselves are part of *iron* and part of *clay ;* for the feet of Nebuchadnezzar's Image, and those of the Fourth Beast, are representative of the same power. The brass, the iron, and the clay, then, are representative of the national elements constituting the power. The Greeks, and the Latins, mixed up with the heterogeneous peoples under the guardianship of the Czar, moulded into form under his imperial sceptre, are the Feet-power that stamps the residue. The residue may be discerned in the names of countries and races hereafter to be confederated under Gōg as their appointed "guard."

While the Feet are occupied in stamping upon Judah and his allies in the glorious land, the Fourth Beast Power and Little Horn of the Goat are fitly represented by the Image Nebuchadnezzar saw in his dream. During the reign of the Clay-Dynasty the image stands upon its Feet for the first time; having incorporated in it, not only Nimroudia and Persia, but the nation of the Greeks, or brazen goats; and " the Holy Roman Empire" and its papal kingdoms, or iron leg and toes.

But, although the Greeks and Latins are all moulded into ONE IMPERIALITY held together by the Miry Clay which gives it form, the distinctiveness of civil and ecclesiastical organization is still preserved. The Two-Horned Beast, the False Prophet, and the Kings of the Earth, are not extinct. The French Empire being transmuted into a Bourbon-kingdom, and the Russian dynasty being on the throne of Constantinople, it becomes the Second horn with Austria of the two-horned symbol. When the Little Horn of the Goat is broken to pieces on the mountains of Israel, the Constantinopolitan Power collapses, being seen no more in the Holy Land for a thousand years. The Two-Horned Beast, the False Prophet, and the Kings of the Earth, are no longer capable of being represented by the Assyrian Image, or Little Horn of the Goat resting upon the territory of the Northern of the Four Horns; because there they will have lost dominion, their jurisdiction after the smiting of the Image by the Stone Power being restricted to Europe, whose Romano-papal constitution these symbols represent.

21. THE HOLY ROMAN DOMINION, OR LITTLE HORN OF THE WEST.

We have seen how the Constantinopolitan Little Horn Power acknowledged the god of guardians, who was unknown to his predecessors under the pagan constitution of the empire. From about A. D. 395 to the recovery and settlement of Italy, A. D. 554, after a war of twenty years, the Roman god flourished in tumultuous times. With the exception of sixty years, the period of the reign of the Gothic kings in Rome, whence they were expelled by the generals of Justinian, his godship was the cherished ally of the Byzantine emperor. During the turbulent period indicated, the Constantinopolitan dominion had receded from Gaul and Spain before the new kingdoms of the West; while the Universal Bishop had been recognized by the barbarian lords of Europe as a god upon earth. This recognition filled him with stoutness towards the emperor, which he would not have ventured to manifest if he had not been energized by their countenance. From A. D. 554 to A. D. 799, Rome had lost her preëminence, having been reduced to the rank of the second city of the Byzantine or Constantinopolitan empire; and

Italy to the condition of a province of it. During this period a violent quarrel broke out between the Roman god and the imperial majesty. The subject of it was *the adoration of images.* The use and even worship of saint-idols was firmly established before the end of the sixth century. In the beginning of the eighth century, however, in the full magnitude of the idolatry, the people of the East were awakened to an apprehension, that under the mask of Christianity they had restored the paganism of their fathers. The Mohammedans, who reigned in Damascus and threatened Constantinople, denounced them as idolaters, whose punishment it was the divine commission of the followers of the Arabian prophet to execute.

It was the invasion of their empire by these avengers of the divine law against images, and the bowing down to them, that stirred up the Orientals to the consideration of the subject, and at length to their opposition to the practice. The monks zealously defended the images, which were also fondly cherished by the clergy and people of Constantinople; while the rude and remote districts of Asia were strangers to the innovation.

In 726, the controversy issued in a revolution. An adventurer named Conora appeared from the mountains of Isauria, filled with zeal and indignation against the images. He was raised to the throne of Constantinople by the Anatolian legions which he commanded, and being installed reigned as the founder of a new dynasty under the imperial name of Leo III., or the Isaurian.

During the first ten years of his reign his policy was moderate and cautious; too much so, indeed, to satisfy the views of the reformers who had effected his elevation. During that period of toil and danger he bowed before the idols he despised, and satisfied the Roman god with the annual profession of his orthodoxy and zeal. But at length their impatience caused him to be more decided. He proscribed the existence as well as the use of religious pictures; the churches of Constantinople and the provinces were cleansed from idolatry; and the images of Christ, the Virgin and the saints, were demolished, or a smooth surface of plaster was spread over the walls of the edifice. The zeal of his party, styled the Iconoclasts, or Image-Breakers, was rendered effective by the cordial coöperation of his five successors, and the East and West were involved in a stormy conflict of one hundred and twenty years. The Iconoclasts, however, were at last suppressed by the Idolaters, who in the reign of the empress Theodora, A. D. 842, finally succeeded in reëstablishing the adoration of the idols of the demons whom they delighted to honor. This system of idolatry continued upwards of six hundred years after, the government and people being sunk in the grossest superstition. "*They repented not of the works of their hands.*" God, therefore, sent against them the Four Euphratean Angels, who at length extinguished their dominion by the capture of Constantinople, A. D. 1453.

While the patient East under the Iconoclast emperors abjured with reluctance her idols, they were fondly cherished and vigorously defended by the independent zeal of the Italians. A distant and dangerous station amidst the barbarians of the West, excited the spirit and freedom of the Bishops of Rome. Their popular election endeared them to the Romans; the public and private indigence was relieved by their ample revenue; and the weakness or neglect of the emperors of Constantinople compelled them to consult, both in peace and war, the temporal safety of the city. In the school of adversity the Roman god insensibly imbibed the qualities and ambition of a prince; so that after the loss of her legions and provinces, the genius and fortune of the popes again restored the supremacy of Rome. "It is agreed," says Gibbon, "that in the eighth century, their dominion was founded on rebellion, and that the rebellion was produced and justified by the heresy of the Iconoclasts:" in other words, that *the temporal power of the popes is based upon a determined adhesion to the worship of demons and of their idols of gold and silver, wood and stone.*

Pope Gregory II., the founder of the papal monarchy, commenced the controversy with Leo the Isaurian, who avowed his intention of breaking the images in Rome; and of transporting the pope in chains and exile to Constantinople if he did not submit to the imperial edict, which abolished the images of Christ, and the Virgin, and of the angels, martyrs, and saints, in all the churches of Italy. The Italians swore to live and die in the defence of the pope, and of the images of his guardian saints. Leo despatched an army into Italy to establish his decree, but being defeated by the idolaters with great slaughter, the edict could not be enforced. This was a great triumph for the Roman god. He convened a synod of anti-Iconoclastic bishops, with whose consent he pronounced a general excommunication against all who should by word or deed attack the tradition of the fathers and the images of the saints. The emperor, of course, was tacitly involved in the sentence, though the god of Roman thunder did not make a personal application of it to Leo. His moderation delayed and prevented the election of a new emperor for Italy and the West; and the Italians were exhorted not to separate from the body of the Roman monarchy; so that till the imperial coronation of Charlemagne, the government of Rome and Italy was exercised *in the name* of the successors of Constantine.

Rome was now free from the foreign yoke of emperor or king; but reduced to her ancient territory from Viterbo to Terracina, and from Narni to the mouth of the Tiber. Her ruins presented the sad image of depopulation and decay: her previous slavery was a habit, her liberty an accident; the effect of superstition, and the object of her own amazement and terror. By the necessity of their situation, her inhabitants were cast into the rough model of a republican government. The style of "the Roman Senate and People" was revived, but the spirit was fled; and their new independence was disgraced by the tumultuous conflict of licentiousness and oppression. The want of laws was supplied by their religion, and their foreign and domestic counsels were moderated by the authority of the Bishop, whom they became accustomed to consider as the first magistrate or prince of the city.

Here then was formed the *nucleus* of A NEW POWER, consisting of a god upon earth, and a scanty remnant, the offspring of slaves and strangers, inhabitants of Rome and its territory; feeble, unwarlike, and despicable in the eyes of the victorious barbarians. As often as the Franks or Lombards expressed their most bitter contempt of a foe, they called him a Roman; "and in this name," says the bishop Luitprand, "we include whatever is base, whatever is cowardly, whatever is perfidious, the extremes of avarice and luxury, and every vice that can prostitute the dignity of human nature." Such were the pope's children at the origin of his principality, a fitting progeny for such a sire. The Lombards were his immediate neighbors, and under their king Astolphus, the equal enemy of the pope and emperor. The love of arms and rapine were congenial to them; and both the prince and people were irresistibly tempted by the disorders of Italy, the nakedness of Rome, and the unwarlike profession of her new chief. They summoned the city to acknowledge the victorious Lombard as her lawful sovereign; and to pay an annual tribute of a piece of gold as the ransom of each citizen, and the sword of destruction was unsheathed to exact the penalty of her disobedience.

Had the pope and his Romans been left to their own resources in this extremity, the world might never have witnessed among the ten barbaric kingdoms of Europe, a power answering to the "*Little Horn with* EYES *like the eyes of a man, and a* MOUTH *speaking great things*," as seen by Daniel on the head of the Fourth Beast. The little popedom was too feeble to defend itself against its rapacious neighbors; so that if succor could not have been procured from a stronger power, it must have perished in the alpha of its existence. In this event, it would be impossible to say what would have been the constitution of Europe for a thousand years past. This, however, may be considered as certain, "the Holy Roman Empire" would never have existed; and "the Saints" would have escaped that long and terrible war by which they have been prevailed against in all the countries of its dominion. But "the powers that be are ordained of God" with reference to an end appointed. He scourges the wicked with the evil works of their own hands. They founded the papacy, which has whipped them who with it warred against the saints with scorpions; while he has overruled its policy to the formation of a situation which will favor the manifestation of his righteousness and power.

In their distress the "strange god" and his feeble folk sought the protection of the king of the French. The ambassadors of Pepin and of the Greek emperor accompanied the pope to the court of Astolphus, king of the Lombards, to persuade him to peace and amity with the papists. But he would listen to nothing short of absolute submission to his sceptre, which would have been fatal to the ambition of the popes. Finding nothing could be done, Stephen III. hastened to Pepin to excite his pity for St. Peter's patrimony, and his indignation against Astolphus who was ready to devour it. Prompted by the love of glory and superstition, Pepin yielded to the solicitation of the Roman Bishop, and proclaimed himself the champion of the papal church. Being the first of the Barbarian Kings who stood up in defence of the "Holy See," the king of France came to be honored by the popes with the title of "Eldest Son of the Church." An alliance was formed between France and the Little Papacy; which in forty-six years from Stephen's visit to Pepin expanded into the Roman Empire of the West, called "*the Holy Roman Empire,*" and represented by the Little Horn of Daniel's Fourth Beast.

From A. D. 754 to A. D. 799 at Christmas, was the period occupied in the establishment of the Little Horn power; which, like the Little Horn of the Goat, budded forth upon the territory of the Kingdom of Babylon, but confined to its western division. The first event in the formation of the Little Horn of the West was the overthrow of Leo the Isaurian's army against the saint-idols of Rome and Italy; the next was the recognition of Charles Martel and his heirs as Patricians of Rome; the assumption of the championship of the papal church by Pepin; his coronation by the pope; and his compulsion of Astolphus to restore its possessions, and to respect its sanctity: the third series of events was the plucking up by the roots of the Lombard kingdom by Charlemagne, the son of Pepin, A. D. 774; his investment with the honors of Patrician, being presented with the keys of the shrine of St. Peter as a pledge and symbol of sovereignty; and with a holy banner which it was their right and duty to unfurl in defence of the church and city: and his coronation by the pope, the people shouting "Long life and victory to Charles, the most pious Augustus, crowned by God the great and pacific emperor of the Romans!" The patrimony of St. Peter was enlarged through the liberality of Pepin and Charlemagne, by the spoliation of the Lombards and the emperor of Constantinople, to the dimensions of an earthly kingdom of respectable limits, constituting the Eye and Mouthship proper of the Roman god. The gift of this enlarged estate did not, however, alienate it from the empire of Charlemagne; for in his life and death, Ravenna and Rome were numbered in the list of his metropolitan cities.

At this crisis of affairs, then, there existed on the territory of the Kingdom of Babylon *Two Little Horn Powers*, THE STRANGE GOD, *and the Ten Horn or Toe Kingdoms.* I would remark here in passing that it has hitherto been found impossible to define these kingdoms according to the number given. Several tens have been guessed at, but the lists bear inaccuracy on the face of them. The solution of the difficulty I believe is this. The kingdoms are represented by *ten horns,* and *ten toes,* not because there would be that precise number on the territory of the Roman Beast between A. D. 476 and A. D. 799, the interval between the fall and restoration of the Western Roman Empire when the kingdoms first appeared; but because that at the time of the revelation of Jesus Christ and the Saints, there will then be ten kingdoms whose territories will embrace those of the original Gothic kingdoms and probably more beside. The ten kingdoms contemporary with the smiting of the Image by the Stone-power, or with the slaying and burning of the Fourth Beast by the Saints, in relation to the old Gothic kingdoms, are as so many trees to their original sapling-roots: the roots may have been originally many more or fewer than the roots of the trees in after ages. The roots planted will be counted by the number of trees expected, and not by the radicles that compose the plants. The Gothic kingdoms of the period indicated were the roots of the present kingdoms, which are designated in prophecy by the number of Romano-Gothic kingdoms extant when the end comes. There will then be ten, neither more nor less; therefore, without regard to their numerical variation in previous ages, they are styled the ten kingdoms of the Beast.

22. "THE TIME OF THE END."

The revelator having pointed out to Daniel the characteristic marks, by which the Little-Horn-of-the-Goat-Power might be known, directs his attention to what should happen to it "*at the time of the end,*" which is the "time appointed" for the *dénouement* or issue to which the whole prophecy of Daniel points. Habakkuk had a vision of the catastrophe; and in noting it down said, "*at the end* it shall speak, and not lie:" and because the truth of the matter would not be discovered till then, Daniel was told to "Shut up the words and seal the book to the time of the end, . . . for the words are closed up and sealed till the time of the end."

The time of the end, then, is the period of the opening and unsealing of the words of the book; so that it may speak intelligibly to "the wise." The opening and unsealing is effected by the events of the time, being an unmistakable fulfilment of what is written; so that every one of "*the wise*" cannot fail to understand.

The time of the end has its beginning, and ending; and period intermediate between the beginning and the ending. Its commencement is marked by an event connected with Egypt; and its ending by a consummation connected with Israel. The fortieth verse of the eleventh chapter announces its beginning by informing the reader that "*at the time of the end shall the King of the South push at him.*" For the southern horn of the Goat to push at him is for the Egyptian Power to attack the Little Horn Power; for "the king" or Little Horn of the Goat is the power last discoursed of in the preceding context. This attack, then, upon the Ottoman *régime* of the kingdom of Babylon, by the King of Egypt, indicates the beginning of the Time of the End. The conclusion of it is marked by the event predicted in the seventh verse of the last chapter, which is to be completed at the end of "a time, times, and an half," and noted in the words, "*When he shall have accomplished to scatter the power of the holy people, all these things shall be finished.*" Between these two orders of events, the attack of Egypt on the Porte and the reconcentration of the power of the Twelve Tribes, *the vision speaks*, and no more of the book of Daniel remains to be fulfilled—the Time of the End will have passed away, in other words, with the establishment of the Kingdom of God.

The reader, on turning to the eleventh chapter, will notice that no more is said about the King of the South, or of Egypt, after the ships of Chittim interfered in his behalf against Antiochus, the King of the North, until the fortieth verse. Between the first event of this verse, then, and that of the thirtieth is an interval of 2006 years. During this long time no note is made of Egypt in the prophecy, nor of the King of the North from the time of the Maccabees, through whom Judah was "holpen with a little help"—verse 34. The connecting link in the prophetic chain between B. C. 160 and A. D. 1838 is the Little Horn of the Goat, which incorporated the Assyrian kingdom of the north, and the kingdom of the south into its own dominion. But in the year 1829, Egypt, which had been so long in vassalage to the Little Horn, or Constantinopolitan power, revolted; and reappeared on the map of the Babylonian world as a kingly power. Mehemet Ali then established himself as king of the south. He attacked and conquered Syria, and for a time was lord ascendant of the east. This exaltation opened new prospects to Mehemet, and he aspired to the throne of the Sultan. The time of the end was just at hand, there being only about four years and a quarter of the evening-morning of 2300 years to expire. In 1838 he "*pushed at*" the Sultan. Hitherto he had confined his operations to Egypt and Syria, but now at the closing of the war he pushed for Constantinople, and advanced as far as Smyrna; and but for the interference of Russia, Austria, Prussia, and England, unconsciously "to establish the vision," he would doubtless have dethroned him. Wearied of this state of affairs, these powers undertook to establish peace, and to place things on a permanent footing. They ordered the king of the south to surrender Syria including Palestine to the sovereignty of the Little Horn, and to restore its fleet which had revolted from the Sultan during the war. Mehemet refused to do either, contending that Syria was his as a part of his kingdom by right of conquest for ever, and the fleet as the spoils of war. These four powers, however, were not to be trifled with. They were willing that the throne of Egypt should be hereditary in his family; but resolved that he should only be Pacha of Syria for life. But the king of the south would not yield, and the result was that the allied fleet under Sir Charles Napier bombarded the cities of the Syrian sea-board, and took possession of St. Jean d'Acre. They again offered him "all that part of Syria, extending from the Gulf of Suez to the Lake of Tiberias, together with the province of Acre for life," if he would restore the Little Horn's fleet. But he still refused, and in the autumn of 1840, they compelled the Egyptians to evacuate the country, and determined he should not have it at all; and threatened that if he did not restore the fleet in ten days, they would make Alexandria too hot to hold him. Prudence, said to be the better part of valor, at length overcame the obstinacy of the king of the south; he therefore yielded, and surrendered the ships within the time. Thus, the Holy Land was wrested from the King of Egypt and restored to the sovereignty of the Constantinopolitan Little Horn, which still continues to possess the country.

Such was the important series of events which marked the approaching termination of the 2300 years, and the commencing of the Time of the End. The king of the south's pushing at "the king" terminating in the disposal of the Holy Land is evidential of the time having arrived to which Jehovah refers in Lev. xxvi. 42, saying, "*I will remember my Covenant* with Abraham, Isaac, and Jacob, and *I will remember the land.*" The king of the south claimed the land as his for ever; but Jehovah hath said, "The land shall not be sold for ever; for *the land is mine.*" If then the God of Israel would not permit the people of his own nation to alienate it from one to another for ever, he would be far from permitting a Gentile power to possess it, or the Allies to grant it him, for ever. The hand of Jehovah may be clearly discerned in the events of this epoch. He hardened the King of Egypt's heart not to accept the land on any other terms than his own, which were certain not to be granted. If they had yielded to his demand, the present "*eastern question,*" involving the overthrow of the Ottoman dynasty of the Little Horn, could not have been created. If the Allies had allowed the king of the south to retain possession of the Holy Land, the Frog-Power could have made no demands on the Sultan for the protectorate of the Holy Places. The application must have been made at Alexandria instead of Constantinople, which would have deprived Russia of the power of interference, having no access to Egypt by land, and her fleets being shut up in the Baltic and Black Sea. But in 1840 the time had come for Jehovah to remember the land; in other words, to put things in train for "*avenging the holy,*" which had been so long trodden under foot of the worst of the

Gentiles. It was necessary, therefore, to place the land under the sovereignty of the Porte, so that when the question of the Holy Places should be mooted by the Frog-Power, it might stir up the King of the North to jealousy, and bring him into collision with the Little Horn. The transfer, then, of the land from Egypt to the Porte prepared the way for the demands of the Frog-Power on the Sultan; the granting of these stirred up the King of the North to send Menschikoff to pick a quarrel with the Sultan, who having rejected his demands found it necessary to prepare for the worst. Meantime the king of the north crossed the Pruth, and took up his position in the Moldo-Wallachian principalities of the Little Horn. It is clear, then, that as far as statesmanship is concerned, the attack of the Allied Powers on Egypt in 1840, and their restitution of the Holy Land to the Porte, was a great political blunder. They should have left it in the possession of the King of the South, or have given it to the Jews under their joint protectorate, and the present Eastern Question, with all its terrible consequences, would never have occurred. But their counsel was turned into foolishness by Jehovah, whose purposes are diametrically opposed to theirs. Their purpose is *to establish Gentile sovereignty over the East for ever;* while, on the contrary, Jehovah's avowed intention is *to restore the kingdom of Israel with dominion over the world.* These projects are as opposite as the poles, and each project has its policy. The European Powers have unsheathed the sword, that the purpose of the strongest may be established. The West is sanguine of speedy and entire success. The boastings of England and France are premature. When they don their armor Powers no more than men should boast; it is time enough for that when they come to put it off. Woefully will these western powers be deceived in the result of the coming struggle. The Ottoman empire will be dried up, and "the sick man" must die in spite of all their efforts to save him. The sure word of prophecy is against them, and shines upon their patient's doom as near, sudden, and complete. He is already *in articulo mortis,* and his efforts but the convulsive energies of an expiring man.

The 2300 years having terminated in 1843, we are now in the eleventh year of the time of the end. The events predicted from the fortieth verse of this chapter to the second verse of chapter twelve all belong to the time of the end, and are yet future. The king of the north is to come against the Little Horn king, and to sweep away the reigning dynasty; many countries are to be overthrown; the land of Egypt will be taken from its Mohammedan rulers; the Holy Land will be invaded by the northern king; his power will be broken there; the nations will be in such trouble as they were never in before; the Lord Jesus Christ will appear on earth; the dead will be raised, and the righteous glorified; and the Kingdom of God established on the ruin of the Kingdom of Men. These are speaking events, trumpet-tongued proclaiming the purpose of Jehovah in all his doings among the children of men.

23. THE KING OF THE NORTH.

The eighth, ninth, and eleventh chapters of Daniel are principally a symbolical and descriptive prophecy concerning *three* of the five horns of the Grecian Goat in their relation to one another so far as their acts and policy affect the fortunes of Judah and the Holy Land. These three horns are the *southern* or Egyptian Horn, the *northern* or GRECO-ASSYRIAN HORN, and its conjunct, the Little Horn, which arose out of it, and will ere long subside into it, the power it represents being absorbed into it by forcible incorporation.

The Greco-Assyrian Horn Power, as we have already seen, was in its origin the Kingdom of Babylon incorporated with the Alexandrian Empire, afterwards acquired by the Seleucidæ, and by this dynasty surrendered to the Romans about sixty-five years before Christ. Till A. D. 324, ROME was exclusively the throne of the Greco-Assyrian Kingdom of Babylon; but from that date until the fall of the Western Empire about A. D. 476, the Power was enthroned in Rome and Constantinople, the former city being the place of the Senate and of the junior emperor, while the latter was the palatial residence of the chief. On the re-conquest of Italy from the Goths in the reign of Justinian, Rome was reduced to the rank of the second city of the Greco-Assyrian, or Constantinopolitan, dominion; but still retained her ecclesiastical preëminence, being the throne of the Chief Pontiff of the Kingdom of Babylon.

On the revival of the Latin empire of the west under Charlemagne, the separation between the East and West became complete. The Constantinopolitan continued the *Greco-Assyrian Dragon-power*, but deprived of its jurisdiction and authority over the West. This surrender of dominion to the New Confederacy of the West is apocalyptically represented in the saying, "*And the Dragon gave him his power, and his throne, and great authority;*"[1] but what he retained was Greek and Assyrian.

This blending of the Romano-Greek power with the Assyrian is the reason why the Little Horn of the Goat is represented as coming out of one of its four horns. They occupy one and the same territory; that is, where the Seleucidian dynasty once ruled, the Little Horn's dynasties afterwards ruled; and where the Little Horn's present dynasty now rules, a Russian dynasty from the north will be established; so that when this form of things obtains, the northern horn and the Little Horn will be blended into *one power*, still Constantinopolitan, but with a Russian instead of an Ottoman for its chief.

But before this can be accomplished these words to Daniel must be fulfilled: "*And the King of the North shall rush on like a tempest against him with chariots and horsemen, and with many ships; and he shall enter into countries and overwhelm and pass over.*" This plainly intimates war between the two horns in the time of the end; and such a war too that will sweep all before the King of the North. He will rush on against him both by land and sea, his forces being distinguished by their numerical strength in "chariots," or *artillery*, cavalry, and ships. The result of this tornado will be a successful one, for he will "*overwhelm and pass over.*"

While I write this, war is not only declared between the two horns, but the northern one has advanced against the Little Horn Dynasty. At present the forces of the King of the North occupy the Danubian Principalities, and positions between the Black Sea and the Caspian. The attack, however, answering to the words of the prophecy has not yet commenced, the affair at Sinope being a mere foretaste by way of illustration of what is yet to come. All the world is prophesying the overthrow of the King of the North, and the impossibility of his doing any thing with his ships against the combined fleets of the Little Horn's allies! It is probable that if the hostile fleets were to come into collision the Russian fleet would be swallowed up; but the Czar is not likely to venture upon so hazardous an experiment. He has only to bide his time, and to look out for eventualities. The elements have interposed for Russia in a greater extremity than the present; and we know it is written, "*Thou breakest the ships of Tarshish with an east wind.*"[2] In the absence of this, however, complications will doubtless arise in the West, which may divert the attention of the Ottoman's allies from the Euxine. This diversion will be Russia's opportunity; and when seized, the movement of the King of the North will answer to the full force of the prophetic word.

The tempest, then, is gathering. The King of the North is mustering his hosts, and fortifying Sevastopol for the protection of his ships against the Anglo-French

(1) Rev. xiii. 2.   (2) Ps. xlviii. 7.

fleet until the time arrives to use them with effect. The Turks have assembled their armies, and the French and English are gathering their forces together for a participation in the conflict. But, nevertheless, things are not yet ripe. The neutrality of Prussia, Austria, and Germany yet delays the rushing forth of the storm in all its violence. Something must arise to cause these powers to declare themselves on one side or the other. Prussia and Austria fear the autocrat, and the volcanic elements of their own dominions, and have no love for the ruler of the French. Maritime disasters, revolutionary outbreaks, or Russian appeals to their dynastic interests and fears, will necessitate their abandonment of neutrality in favor of the king of the north. The division of the Kingdom of Babylon into two belligerent sections will then be complete, and Russia will be impregnable. The rush of nations then ensuing will be terrific, and is well described by the prophet— who says, "Hark! a multitude of many peoples making an uproar as the noise of seas. Hark! a tumult among peoples, warring as a tumult of mighty waters; they rage against peoples like a roar of many waters."[1] This is Isaiah's description of things "when the nations are angry,"[2] and the king of the north rushes on like a tempest against the Little Horn. At present it is only the gathering of the storm, but when fairly begun, who can say with effect, "Peace, be still?"

The king of the north's career for a time will be most successful. Some of the countries he is to enter into and overwhelm are Egypt and the Goodly Land. "He shall send forth his hand upon countries: and the land of Egypt shall not escape. But he shall have power over the treasures of gold and of silver, and over all the precious things of Egypt: and the Libyans and Ethiopians shall be at his steps." These are the forty-second and forty-third verses, and explain somewhat the passage in the fortieth, that "He shall enter into the countries, and shall overwhelm and pass over." Then follows the saying in the forty-first verse, "He shall enter also into the goodly land." To do what is foretold of him in regard to Egypt implies the conquest of Turkey; because not being a maritime power he cannot get at Egypt and Palestine until he first overwhelm the Ottoman.

The last country he will invade will be the Holy Land; whose covenanted limits are from "the entering in to Hamath" to the Nile, for its western frontier; and from thence by the Red Sea to the Persian Gulf for its south line; and from the Gulf along the Euphrates to the mountains of Amanus for its eastern side. He will not be able to occupy the whole country, the south and south-east of it being held by his antagonists; for it is written in the prophecy, "*But these shall escape out of his hand, Edom, and Moab, and the chief of the children of Ammon;*" the reason of their escape being because they will then be in the hands of a powerful antagonist.

24. PROOF OF THE RUSSIAN POWER BEING THE KING OF THE NORTH.

The proof lies in the obvious identity that exists between Daniel's "king of the north" of *the time of the end*, and Ezekiel's "Gog" of *the latter days*. By comparing what is said about each of these in the two prophets, it will be manifest that they can only be different titles for the same power. The following particulars may be cited in proof:

1. Their geographical position is the same. Gog's country is the north parts in relation to the Holy Land; as it is written, "*Thou shalt come from thy place out of the north parts.*" Gog is therefore king of the north, his *place* or country being there.

2. They are both the adversaries of Israel, and the invaders of their country. The eleventh chapter of Daniel abundantly proves this in relation to the king of

---

(1) Isai. xvii. 12.　　(2) Rev. xi. 18.

the north; and of Gog, Jehovah says, "*Thou shalt come up against my people Israel, as a cloud to cover the land.*"

3. The time they invade the land is the same. The king of the north invades it *in the time of the end;* and of Gog it is said, "*It shall be in the latter days, and I will bring thee against my land.*"

4. The same peoples are named as components of their armies. The Libyans and Ethiopians are at the steps of the king of the north; and in the enumeration of Gog's forces, it says, "*Persia, Ethiopia, and Libya with them.*"

5. Hostile tidings come from the east and north which excite the king of the north to fury; while tidings also come to Gog from the same quarter to deter him from invading the Holy Land.

6. The king of the north encounters the Little Horn; and Gog is antagonized by "*Sheba and Dedan, and the merchants of Tarshish and the young lions thereof*"—the Anglo-Indian power—now in alliance with the Little Horn.

7. They both meet with the same fate, at the same time, in the same place, and by the same power. The "*king of fierce countenance*" stands up against the Prince of princes; the *king of the north* encounters Michael the Great Prince; and *Gog* is smitten by the Lord God. They all three come to their end with none to help them; they all fall upon the mountains of Israel, and consequent upon their overthrow Israel is delivered.

These seven particulars prove that Gog and the king of the north are but different titles for the same power; and the title given to Gog in the thirty-eighth and thirty-ninth chapters of Ezekiel proves that this northern power is no other than the Russian. In these places the prophet is addressed by Jehovah as the representative of Him who is to vanquish Gog and to deliver Israel. Hence, he says to him, "*Son of Man, set thy face against Gog, the land of Magog, prince of Rosh, Meshekh, and Thuval, and prophesy against him.*" In this title to the prophecy the antagonists are indicated, namely, the Son of Man (*ben-adam*) or Seed of the Woman, on the one side; and the Prince of Rosh, the Head of the Serpent-power, on the other. Hence, by understanding Gog's title, the reader may know which of "the powers that be" is chosen of God to personate the Serpent's Head when it is bruised by the Woman's Seed.

The question as to what nations are signified by Rosh, Meshekh, and Thuval, has been long since determined by the learned. The celebrated Bochart about the year 1640, observed, in his elaborate researches into Sacred Geography, that $P\Omega\Sigma$, *Rōs*, or ראש, *Rōsh*, is the most ancient form under which history makes mention of the name of Russia; and he contended that *Rosh* and משך, *Měshkěh*, properly denote the nations of Moscovy and Russia. "It is credible," says he, "that from Rosh and Meshekh (that is, the Rhossi and Moschi) of whom Ezekiel speaks, descended the Russians and Muscovites, nations of the greatest celebrity in European Scythia." We have indeed ample and positive testimony, that the Russian nation was called $P\Omega\Sigma$, *Rōs*, by the Greeks in the earliest period in which we find it mentioned, as, Εθνος δε οι Ρως Σκυθικον περι τον αρκτωον Ταυρον; that is, "*the Rosh are a Scythian nation bordering on the northern Taurus.*" And their own historians say, "It is related that the Russians (whom the Greeks called Ρως, and sometimes Ρωσος, *Rōsos*) derived their name from Ros, a valiant man, who delivered his nation from the yoke of its tyrants."

Thus then we discern the modern names of Russia and Moscow in the Bible names adduced. It is not difficult also to recognize in תובל, Thuvahl, or *Tubl*, or as the Greeks wrote it Θοβελ, *Thobel*, a name which naturally connects itself with them; and which in conjunction with them tends in a very remarkable manner to determine and fix the *proper object* of the prediction. The river Tobol gives name to the city of Tobol*ium*, or Tobol*ski*, the metropolis of the extensive region of Siberia, lying immediately eastward of the territories of Muscovy. *Thobol* and

M'sh'kl, are mentioned together by Ezekiel, who characterizes them as nations trading in copper;[1] a metal which, it is notorious, abounds in the soil of Siberia; a region which includes all the northern part of Asia which borders on Russia to the west, on the Ice-sea to the north, on the Eastern Ocean on the east, and on Great Tartary to the south. And thus the three denominations Rosh, Meshekh, and Thuval, united in the prophecy, point out, with equal capacity and conciseness, those widely extended regions which at the present day, we denominate collectively THE RUSSIAN EMPIRE.

Gog is styled the "*Prince of Rosh, Meshekh, and Thuval,*" that is, Autocrat of the Russians, Muscovites, and Siberians, or of "*All the Russias.*" But he is also styled "Gog of the land of Magog" as well. There must be something significant in this. It affirms that he is sovereign of Magog as well as prince of all the Russias; for there in the latter days is his proper dominion. "Whoever reads Ezekiel," says Michaelis, "can hardly entertain a doubt that Gog is the name of a sovereign, and Magog that of his people; the prophet speaks of the former, not as a people, but as *an Emperor.*" Let us then now inquire where is the region styled Magŏg; that we may be able to ascertain of what people besides the Russians, Gog will be the imperial *mishmar*, or sentinel. And as Gomer is represented by Ezekiel as a constituent of his confederacy, we will also endeavor to establish what people among the moderns will answer to the name.

From the Hebrew Scriptures we learn that Magog and Gomer were the names of two of the sons of Japheth; and it is to ancient Hebrew authority alone that we can resort to ascertain where, according to the common repute of the Israelites, the nations which descended from these two heads of families, and which *long retained the proper names* of those heads, were spread and established. Josephus says, "that Japheth, the son of Noah, had seven sons; who proceeding from their primitive seats in the mountains of Taurus and Amanus, ascended Asia to the river Tanais (or Don;) and then entering Europe penetrated as far westward as the Straits of Gibraltar, occupying the lands which they successively met with in their progress; all of which were uninhabited; and bequeathed their names to their different families or nations. That Gomer founded the Gomari, whom the Greeks at that time called *Galatæ*—τους νυν ὑφ Ἑλληνων Γαλλατας καλουμενους;—and that Magog founded the Magogæ, whom the Greeks then call *Scythæ*—σκυθαι." It only therefore remains for us to ascertain, which were the nations that the Greeks in the time of Josephus called *Scythæ*, and which they then styled *Galatæ*; and to observe whether the geographical affinities of these nations are such as answer to those which are plainly required by the prophecy for Magog and Gomer.

Herodotus, the most ancient Greek writer accessible, acquaints us "that the name Scythæ was a name given by the Greeks to an ancient and widely-extended people of Europe, who had spread themselves from the river Tanais, or Don, westward along the banks of the Ister or Danube." "The Greeks," observes Major Rennel, "appear to have first used the term Scythia in its application to their neighbors the Scythians of the Euxine, who were also called *Getæ*, or *Gothi*; and were those who afterward subdued the Roman empire: and from which original stock the present race of people in Europe seem to be descended." And again: "The Scythians of Herodotus appear to have extended themselves in length from Hungary, Transylvania, and Wallachia, on the westward, to the river Don on the eastward." Thus the testimony of Herodotus and Josephus is in perfect agreement concerning the progress of Magog and Gomer. In these same regions the Scythæ continued many ages after Herodotus, and even long after the time of Josephus; for Dio Cassius, who lived 150 years after Josephus, and about 200 after Christ, relates that Pompey in his return into Europe from Asia, "determine

---

(1) Ezek. xxvii. 13.

to pass to the Ister, or Danube, through the Scythæ, and so to enter Italy." These were the original Scythæ. But Herodotus states further, that a portion of the same people in an after age, turned back upon the European seats of their fathers, and established themselves in Asia; and from these sprung the Asiatic Scythæ, who in process of time almost engrossed the name to themselves.

Since the name of Scythæ, or Magog, is to be considered not by itself, but in geographical connection with Galatæ, or Gomer, we have only to inquire, whether any geographical affinity is really ascribed by the Greeks to the Scythæ and Galatæ? and to ascertain to what regions of the earth those names so associated were applied. If we can discover these two points, we ought thereby to have discovered specifically the Magog of the prophecy, which is to be associated with the region, or people, of Gomer.

Diodorus Siculus, who lived about a century before Josephus, traces them much further into Europe than the Danube; *even to the shores of the Baltic, and to the very confines of the Galatæ of the Greeks*. In speaking of the amber found upon the shores of that sea, he there places the region expressly denominated, "*Scythia above or north of Galatia*." In which description we at length find the Scythæ, or Magogæ, in the immediate neighborhood of the Galatæ of the Greeks, or Gomer.

GALATIA—Γαλατια—is the common and familiar name used by all the earlier Greek historians for *Gaul*, the Gallia of the Latins; and Galatæ—Γαλαται—is the common Greek name for Gauls, or the Galli of the Latins. Thus Strabo says, "*all the Galatæ were called Celtæ by the Greeks;*" and it is equally true that "the Celtæ were called Galatæ by the Greeks, and Galli by the Latins." To inquire, who were "the Galatæ of the Greeks?" is therefore the same as to inquire who were the Galli of the Romans? A colony of these Galatæ or Galli in the third century before Christ, emigrated from Gaul and established themselves in Asia Minor; where they were ever after called by their Greek name, Galatians. Diodorus' "*Scythia above Gaul extending towards the Baltic*," accurately describes that large tract of Europe above the Rhine, or *northern boundary of Gaul*, through which flow the rivers Elbe, Ems, and Weser. Here, and in the countries immediately adjoining, were *the* SCYTHÆ *bordering upon the* GALATÆ *on the north;* that is to say, a considerable part of MAGOG *geographically associated with* GOMER.[1] Diodorus elsewhere describes the northern part of Galatia, or Gaul, as *confining upon Scythia*. "The Greeks," says he, "call those who inhabit Marseilles and the inland territory, and all those who dwelt towards the Alps and Pyrenean mountains, by the name of Celts; but those who occupy the country lying to the northward, between the Ocean and the Hyrcynian mountain, and all others as far as Scythia, they denominate Galatæ; but the Romans call all those nations by one collective appellation, Galatæ, that is, Galli." These geographical affinities unite in the name of Celto-Scythæ, mentioned by Strabo. "The ancient Greeks," says he, "at first called the northern nations by the general name of Scythians; but when they became acquainted with the nations *in the west*, they began to call them by the different names of Celts, and Celto-Scythæ;" and again, "the ancient Greek historians called the northern nations collectively Scythians and Celto-Scythæ;" which latter name plainly denoted the most western portion of the Scythæ, adjoining Gaul; of the number of whom were the Scythæ on the north of the Galatæ, or the Σκυθαι υπερ Γαλατιαν.

In this general description may be easily discerned that extended portion of *the West of Europe*, comprehending ancient Gaul, Belgium, and the countries bordering upon them, which constituted in our day the Napoleon empire. *Gomer, then, points immediately to France*. "Scythia above Gaul," or *Magog above Gomer*, that

---

(1) Gomer, ex quo Galatæ, id est, Galli; that is to say, "Gomer, from whom proceeded the Galatæ, that is, the Gauls."—Isidor Origin, lib. ix. He wrote about A. D. 400.

is, to the north of it, through which flows the Ems, Elbe, and Weser, is the country from which proceeded principally that renowned people who in the early ages of Romanism formed an extensive confederacy with their kindred nations upon the Rhine, which had migrated successively thither from the regions of the Danube; and who under the common denomination of FRANKS overran Gaul, and subdued it; and finally establishing their power and population in the conquered country, permanently superseded the name of Gaul by that of FRANCE. "As for the seats of the Franks," says the Universal History, " it appears from their constant incursions into Gaul, that they dwelt on the banks of the Rhine in the neighborhood of Mentz. All historians speak of them as placed there till their settling in Gaul. Their country, according to the best modern geographers and historians, was bounded on the north by the Ocean and the Rhine; on the south by the Maine; and on the east by the Weser.

These were therefore the Celto-Scythians, or Scythians on the northern confine of Gaul; that is, *Magog in contiguity with Gomer*. The Chaldean interpreter applies the name of Magog to *the Germans*, in short, all the ancients looked for the Magog of scripture in the West. The Scythæ of Asia, who as we have seen were only a partial emigration, or reflux, from their ancient stock in Europe, cannot, with any soundness of criticism, be taken account of in this argument.

From the evidence, then, now before the reader, the proposition may be considered as fairly proved, that Daniel's "*king of the north*" is the same power as Ezekiel's "*Gog;*" and that Gog being the Russian Power in full manifestation, the king of the north and the Russian Power are identical. This position being established, we can now look around us, and far before us into the future, and be prepared to point out assuredly what will be the general progress and issue of the present EASTERN QUESTION.

25. FUTURE MAGNITUDE OF THE CZAR'S DOMINION.

Daniel does not particularize the extent of the dominion of the King of the North in the eleventh chapter; though indeed he symbolizes it in his second. But what he has omitted in the eleventh, Ezekiel has sufficiently supplied in his prophecy of Gog. By the names of the peoples he mentions in Gog's title, and the description of his army, the reader may learn what nations the Autocrat gathereth and heapeth to himself as *thick clay* in the day of his high-exaltation.[1]

Daniel says of him in general terms, "He shall enter into the countries, and shall overwhelm and pass over"—and "*many* (רֻבּוֹת *ravbōth*, referring to ארצות *arētzōth*, countries, understood) *shall fall;*" that is, from weakness, as the word implies—the worn-out condition of the powers facilitating his progress. Ezekiel tells us that these countries are those of Magog, Gomer, Persia, Ethiopia, Libya and Togarmah, with their hosts; in addition to Rosh, Mĕshĕkh, and Thuval. He says that the King of the North, or Gog, is to be for משמר *mishmar*, a guard sentinel, shepherd, or supervisor, over all these.[2] It is not to be supposed that he will be the sole emperor, or crowned head. The position marked out for him is that of a King of kings, and a Lord of lords, as was his predecessor, Nebuchadnezzar, the post-Nimroudian founder of the Kingdom of Babylon. It is probable that the House of Hapsburg will continue imperial; nay, I would say more than probable. The Autocrat's supervisorship of the Kingdom of Babylon is not at all incompatible with the Western Imperiality of Austria. Nicholas in Constantinople and Francis Joseph in Vienna, or even Rome, with the priority assigned to the former, would only be a resuscitation of an old form of the Kingdom of the Fourth Beast, as when Arcadius and Honorius amicably divided, or rather agreed to sustain *the Majesty of the Two-Legged Iron and Brass dominion* upon the

---

(1) Hab. ii. 5, 6.   (2) Ezek. xxxviii, 7.

united shoulders. According to this arrangement there will then exist *a Beast with Two Horns like the horns of a Lamb, and speaking as a Dragon*,[1] exercising all the power now exercised by the thrones, principalities, and powers, in the countries named by Ezekiel, and represented by the *Ten-Horned* symbol.

The Autocrat, then, as chief emperor, will become in the progress of events "*Lord of the Ascendant,*" even the Agag of the East and West; shining forth from his lofty throne as Lucifer, son of the morning, over the nations weakened by the gratification of his insatiable ambition. If he have not yet said it, the time is coming when he will "think an evil thought,"[2] and say in his heart, as it is revealed of him, "I will ascend into heaven, I will exalt my throne above the stars of God: I will sit also upon the Mount of the Congregation (Zion) in the sides of the north: I will ascend above the heights of the clouds; *I will be like the Most High!*"[3] He who made man, and knows thoroughly the vanity and presumption of the human heart, has spoken thus of the last occupant of the throne of the Kingdom of Babylon. A man of such a soul as this is not upright, and therefore unfit to rule the world for God; for "*He that ruleth over men must be just, ruling in the fear of Jehovah.*"[4] His dominion's duration must therefore of necessity be brief. But while it lasts, he will prove himself to be "a proud man, who enlargeth his desire as the grave, and as death, and cannot be satisfied, but gathereth unto himself all nations, and heapeth unto him all peoples, . . . lading himself with *thick clay.*"[5]

By turning to a map of Europe and Asia, the reader may trace out the territory of the Kingdom of Babylon as it is destined to exist in its last form under the King of the North in his Gogian manifestation. The names of countries furnished by Ezekiel will lead him to a just conception of its general extent. Besides "All the Russias," it will take in Norway, Sweden, Denmark, Holland, Belgium, France, Spain, Portugal, Italy, Switzerland, Germany, Prussia, Austria, Turkey, Persia, Tartary, Greece, the Roman Africa, and Egypt. This will be a dominion of great magnitude, extending from the North Sea to the Wall of China and Affghanistan, and from the Ice-Sea to the Deserts of Africa and Arabia.

26. NEBUCHADNEZZAR'S IMAGE THE SYMBOL OF THE AUTOCRAT'S DOMINION INCLUSIVE OF FRANCE.

The organization which this vast empire will assume, when fully developed, is represented in the second chapter of Daniel by a Colossus in human form, which as an apparition flitted before the mind of Nebuchadnezzar in a dream. Daniel says that *the scene* of which it was the subject, was representative of what should be "*in the Latter Days.*" This being admitted, it follows that what is recorded in that chapter is yet in the future. The scene exhibits a Colossus standing on its feet in unrivalled brightness of glory, and terrible to behold. Standing thus for a time not indicated, another object appears, even A STONE representative of a Power not in mortal hands. This Stone-Power smites the Colossus on the Feet, and it falls; after which the Stone proceeds to *reduce the broken fragments to dust*, which by the violence of the process is carried away so completely that not a vestige of the Colossus remains; and the place left void by the disappearance of the statue becomes the territory of the Stone-power, which by the operation becomes a Mountain-dominion, and fills the whole Image-earth.

This scene has never been exhibited before the eyes of the world, because the constituents of the Colossus have never yet been put together so as to form the Image of the scene. These constituents are represented by the different metalic parts, as the Chaldæo-Assyrian golden head; the Medo-Perics Assyrian

---

(1) Rev. xiii. 11. (2) Ezek. xxxviii. 10. (3) Isai. xiv. 13,14. (4) 2 Sam. xxiii. 3.
(5) Hab. ii. 4–6.

silver arms and breast; the Macedo-Assyrian belly of brass; the Greco-Assyrian, and Greco-Egyptian, northern and southern thighs of brass; the Latino-Assyrian and the Greco-Assyrian eastern and western iron legs; and the Russo-Greek Assyrian and Latino-Assyrian iron and clay feet and toes. Now, while the head, breast and arms, belly, thighs, legs and toes, have all existed, *the Feet have not yet been formed;* so that it has been hitherto impossible for the Colossal Image to stand erect, as Nebuchadnezzar saw it in his dream. It is, therefore, the mission of the Autocrat to *form the feet and set up the image before the world, in all its excellent brightness, and terribleness of form;* that all men subject to the Kingdom of Babylon may worship the work of its creator's power.

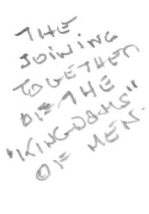

When it stands upon the Plain of Dura the imperial fabric will rest upon the Russo-Greek and Latin Feet and Toes—*two emperors and ten kings* on the Roman earth, whatever may be beyond. The form of the Image necessitates the reduction of the present number of European emperors to a peace establishment. There are but two Legs, therefore there can be only two imperial divisions of the dominion in its latter-day, or time-of-the-end manifestation. From mature consideration I am satisfied that Austria and Russia will be the imperial supporters of the united majesty of the Image; for there must be Ten Kingdoms, and if Austria were suppressed, and France remain imperial, the tenth kingdom would be wanting; besides that prophecy has already designated France as a Gomerian constituent of the Image, and as "*a tenth of the city*" or State of Babylon.[1] From these premises my inference is, that the present Napoleon-empire is simply meteoric. Providence has raised it up as the Frog-Power dominion[2] to work out by its policy an antagonist Russo-Austrian policy leading to the manifestation of the Image, preparatory to the overthrow of the Kingdom of Babylon by the Stone-Power, or kingdom of God. Had the French empire not been resuscitated, events would have flowed in a different channel, and the gathering of the nations to the Armageddon-conflict evaded. State documents prove that the policy of Louis Napoleon has been the exciting cause of the Eastern Question; and it will be the cause of still further complications. But beyond a certain limit he cannot go. He has a mission to perform, and when it is accomplished his work is done. He will not be allowed to settle himself in the throne of a French empire. *The age of conquest,* he says, *is gone, never more to return;* and this is most complacently reëchoed by the present admirers of Louis Napoleon in England. But, how little do the puppets, through whom Providence works out its purposes, understand the times and tendencies to which they belong! They propose, but the disposition of all things is of God. There is to be *no more fighting for conquest or aggrandizement, or selfish advantage between France and England,* says Lord Palmerston; *but for the liberties of oppressed nations, and to establish the freedom and independence of Europe:* and, continues he, "I am confident *it will be crowned with success.*" There may, indeed, be no more fighting between France and England, as belligerent principals: but their leaders are all wrong in supposing that "the age of conquest is past for ever," and that they will succeed in establishing the freedom and independence of Europe. There never has been such an age of conquest as that which is now opening upon the world; and as to the establishment of European freedom and independence, the war they have initiated is the setting in of an overwhelming inundation that will submerge them under one of the most terrible and scorching despotisms that ever wrung the heart of nations. England's ally, in whom she now glories, and by whose aid she proposes to do such great things for Europe, will eventually prove but a broken reed. *The French empire must fall,* and Louis Napoleon give place to a nominee of his "good friend" the Autocrat; for before the end comes the French Monarchy must reäppear; and

---

(1) Rev. xi. 13. (2) Rev. xvi. 13.

then, unless Britain can form some alliance beyond the limits of the Kingdom of Babylon, she will have to fight the battle of freedom and independence alone, and at the price of her own existence if she fail. France, as I have said, is Gomerian; and as such must come under the great Cossack Ruler of the Gogian Image; and then, though not as a principal, she will send her conquered and crest-fallen hosts to do battle for the Autocrat against Britain on the mountains of Israel's land.

It is impossible that Nebuchadnezzar's Image can represent any other imperial confederacy of nations than that under the King of the North in the time of the end. The names given in Ezekiel's list of Gog's army, are representative of the countries known to have existed under the dynastic rule of the gold, the silver, the brass and the iron. Part of Assyria proper already belongs to the King of the North, and pertains to the *gold;* Persia is to be with him as the *silver* element; his Grecism is typified by the *brass;* and his Gomerians by the *iron*, while his Magogians, Roshi, Muscovites, and Siberians, with the Tartars of Togarmah's house, are *the clay*, which he commingles with the iron to form the Feet as the connecting medium between the Legs and Toes. Besides, no two such empires as that of the Image and the Northern Gog could coexist in the latter days; there would be neither population nor space for them in the Kingdom of Babylon. As then the time and place of their existence are the same, they must, therefore, be one and the same confederate power, the image being symbolical or representative of the Gogian dominion of the King of the North, or Autocrat of Russia.

27. EDOM, MOAB, AND AMMON DIVIDED OFF FROM TURKEY FOR A PRICE,

"But these shall escape out of his hand, Edom and Moab, and the chief territory of the sons of Ammon."

These territories are not included in the Gogian empire. They are situated in the south and south-east of the Holy Land, and will fall under the dominion of another power, hostile to the King of the North. It is probable that the power holding these countries will for a time possess Egypt, but in the course of the war lose it; for, "the land of Egypt shall not escape" the King of the North, which implies its independence of him to a certain time.

In the thirty-ninth verse of the eleventh chapter of Daniel, the phrase אדמה יחלק במחיר *ădahmah yĕchăllek bimchir*, is rendered by Moses Stuart, "Land will he distribute as a reward," and affirms it of Antiochus. But a general distribution of land to favorites is no special characteristic, but common to all powers. It is evidently some particular land or country the Little Horn is to treat as expressed by the words. The land is without doubt that which was to be trodden under foot by the Little Horn abomination until the end—the Holy Land.

Now, though the words are susceptible of the rendering he has given, the testimonies of other prophets satisfy me that it is not the proper rendering in this place. I rather incline to the words, "*he shall divide the country for a price,*" as foretelling a bargain and sale between the Little Horn and another power of a portion of the territory now in its possession. Jehovah addressing Israel upon the subject of their restoration, says by Isaiah, "*I gave Egypt for thy ransom, Ethiopia* (Khush) *and Seba for thee.*"[1] Egypt and Khushistan are countries acknowledging the suzerainty of the Porte, and so situated that a line from one to the other would divide off a tract including Edom, Moab, and the chief of the territory of the sons of Ammon; so that while the King of the North is making great progress elsewhere, an adversary is securing a maritime section of Ottomania for itself.

Besides the passage in Isaiah, there is a testimony strikingly to the point in

(1) Isai. xliii. 3.

Joel.[1] Speaking of the time when Jehovah will gather the armies of all nations into the valley of Jehoshaphat, on the east of the Holy City; which encampment there is the same as the King of the North's, "*between the seas to the mountain, the glory of the holy;*" the prophet says, that they will be gathered there for a great overthrow because they have scattered Israel, and *divided Jehovah's land*. The words are in the English version, "*parted my land;*" "parted" being the same word in the Hebrew as "divide" in Dan. xi. 39. In Joel the word for "land" is ארץ *ĕrĕtz*, but in Daniel אדמה *ădāmăh*. Now, though both words are applied to the Holy Land and other countries, I take it that *ădāmăh* in relation to the Little Horn of the Goat, has reference to more country than that of the Holy; while *ĕrĕtz* in Joel refers exclusively to Jehovah's land, which will suffer division or partition as a part of the *ădāmăh* or country bargained for between the Constantinopolitan and his wealthy customer. The partition of countries in general by "the powers that be," is no offence against God, because, although the earth is his and the fulness thereof, yet he does not lay claim to them in that special sense in which he does to Palestine. He has published to the world, "*the Land is mine, and shall not be alienated;*"[2] and because it is his, and all pertaining to it, therefore it is all holy—the land, the cities, the metropolis, and the nation. In relation to the Gentiles, they are under an interdict. They are forbidden to appropriate them, or to oppress and spoil them, under penalty of Jehovah's wrath and terrible indignation. Poland may be divided, and Lombardy and Hungary "plucked up by the roots" with impunity, because they are the lands of Israel's enemies, the worshippers of the Beast that has made war upon the Saints and overcome them; but, woe be to the peoples that divide the Holy, and burden themselves with Jerusalem, "the glory of the Holy." Hear what Jehovah proclaims in regard to this subject: "Behold, I will make Jerusalem a cup of trembling unto all the people round about when they shall be in the siege both against Judah and Jerusalem. And in that day will I make Jerusalem a burdensome stone for all people; all that burden themselves with it shall be cut in pieces, though all the people of the earth be gathered together against it."[3]

The country then divided off by the Constantinopolitan will include the south and south-east of the Holy Land, comprehending Edom, Moab, and the principal part of Ammon. I do not say that this will be all that will be purchased of the Constantinopolitan. I rather expect that all Palestine (which, however, does not comprehend in the modern use of that name all the Holy Land) will be included in the purchase; but what I mean is, that when the seat of war is transferred to the Holy Land, that portion of the purchase anciently styled Edom, Moab, and Ammon, in major part, will be exempted from the fate of Egypt; and therefore form an asylum for refugees from the northern parts of the country. It will be the section preserved from conquest by the power of the purchaser at the time of the King of the North's overthrow by Michael, the great Prince Royal of Israel.

The power that comes into possession of "Tyre and Sidon, and all the coasts of Palestine,"[4] with Edom, Moab, Ammon, Egypt, Khushistan, and Seba, is the great *Latter-Day Antagonist of Gog*, whose dominion attains to the full after the rushing forth the King of the North like a tempest against the Little Horn of the Goat; and because it possesses these countries in "the time of the end," it is the Tyre, or Daughter of Tyre, the Edom, the Moab, and so forth, of the latter days; so that the prophecies treating of those lands at the time, are really delivered concerning that power; for the prophets speak not so much of races and individual potentates, as of powers on the territories named from the ancient founders of states upon them.

Let us take Moab as an illustration. Moab has evidently a latter-day history,

---

(1) Joel iii. 2.   (2) Lev. xxv. 23.   (3) Zech. xii. 2.   (4) Joel iii. 4.

from the notice taken of her in Daniel; and from the saying, "I will bring again the captivity of Moab in the latter days, saith Jehovah."[1] We are not, however, to expect that the real descendants of Lot will return there; for their race is melted down and lost among the nations; but that the country called Moab, now a desolate portion of the Constantinopolitan, or Dragon empire, will be occupied by a power that shall restore prosperity to the country previous to its coming into the possession of the occupant of David's throne, who will make her the washbowl[2] of his kingdom.

When the northern Gog invades the Holy Land and advances against Jerusalem, there will of course be great alarm among the Jewish inhabitants of the country whose especial enemy he is. As the power that overshadows them with its protection is compelled to fall back on Edom, Moab, and Ammon, where it will maintain its position, they will retire with it as "outcasts" from its northern section, which will then be in the hand of Gog the "spoiler," the "extortioner," and the "oppressor" of Judah. Now in view of this situation of affairs, the Spirit of God has oracularized the following address to this Moabitish power, saying, "Take counsel, execute judgment; make thy shadow as the night in the midst of the noonday; hide the outcasts, bewray not him that wandereth. Let mine outcasts dwell with thee, Moab; be thou a covert to them from the face of the spoiler." From this it is evident that in the time of the end the power occupying Moab is antagonist to the spoiler, and the protector of Jehovah's outcasts; which a Moabitish power has never been before. The protection will certainly be accorded until the Deliverer come to Zion. If the power understood the oracle, its energy of resistance would be increased by it; because the exhortation to become the protector of the Jewish outcasts is immediately followed by the announcement, that "the extortioner is at an end, the spoiler ceaseth, and the oppressors are consumed out of the land;" as the result, doubtless, of the king of the north "coming to his end with none to help him." The power occupying Moab, then, would not be disposed to enter into terms with Gog and to deliver up the refugees; but would be stirred up to make greater efforts in hope of more prosperous campaigns than heretofore; assuredly gathering that the overthrow of the enemy was not remote.

The consumption of the oppressors out of the Holy Land can only be coëtaneous with the fall of Gog upon the mountains of Israel by the fury of the Lord God;[3] the overthrow of the king of the north by Michael;[4] the smiting of the Image on the Feet by the Stone; the consumption of Paul's Man of Sin; and the beating down of the Assyrian by the voice of Jehovah.[5] They are all one and the same event happening to the same power—the treading of the winepress in the day of vengeance, when the Hero of Bozrah tramples the people in his anger, and makes them drunk in his fury, and brings down their strength to the earth.[6]

But when it shall be said, the treaders down are consumed out of the Holy Land, what order of things will obtain there from that time forward? Will the Moabitish protector of Judah advance his forces and reöccupy the scene of Gog's disaster; or what other alternative will remain? The answer is, by no means! The oracle of God declares, in this same prophecy concerning Moab, that when the oppressors are consumed out of the land, "The throne shall be established in mercy; and He (whose right it is) shall sit upon it in truth in the tabernacle of David, judging and seeking judgment, and hasting righteousness."[7] When this establishment of the kingdom of David is perfected, Jehovah will have accomplished to scatter the power of the Holy People; an event which marks the terminus of the "*time, times, and a half,*" and finishes the things revealed in Daniel's book.

(1) Jer. xlviii. 47. (2) Ps cviii. 9. (3) Ezek. xxxviii. 18; xxxix. 3, 4. (4) Dan. viii. 25; xi. 45; xii. 1. (5) Isai. xxx. 30, 31. (6) Isai. lxiii. 4, 6. (7) Isai. xvi. 3–5.

28 BRITAIN, THE MOABITISH ANTAGONIST TO RUSSIA IN THE LATTER DAYS.

Gog and the King of the North being the same, and this same having been proved to be the Russian power, it follows that the power hostile to the king of the north and Gog must be Moabitish and the adversary of the Russian. This admitted, the next question would be, What evidence is there that the British power is that Moabitish antagonist? This, then, is the point I now propose to illustrate.

By consulting Daniel and Ezekiel it will be found, that the Gogian King of the North is excited to "great fury," because of the reported movements of an enemy for the purpose of thwarting his designs. Having intimated that the king of the north will invade the Holy Land, Daniel continues: "But tidings out of *the East* and out of *the North* shall trouble him; therefore he shall go forth with great fury to destroy and make away many." From this statement, then, it appears that the power which excites the fury of the king of the north has its station in the east and north relatively to the Holy Land. Without further information than Daniel affords it would be impossible to do more than guess at the name of the power; to relieve us therefore of this uncertainty the Spirit has informed us by Ezekiel in what countries of the east and north the troubling power may be found.

After telling us that in the latter days Gog shall come against the mountains of Israel like a storm-cloud to cover the land, Ezekiel informs us, that this invasion will be the result of his conceiving a mischievous purpose, or "thinking an evil thought." He then reveals to us the tenor of this evil thought which fills the heart of the Autocrat, which is notably foreshadowed by his present policy. "I will go up to the land of unwalled villages," he will say; "to take a spoil, and to take a prey; and to turn my hand upon the reinhabited desolations, and upon the people gathered out of the nations which have gotten cattle and goods, that dwell in *the midst* of the land." He resolves to turn spoiler, extortioner, and oppressor of those Jews who will then have resettled "the tenth"[1] which is to be repeopled and browsed. The Gogian King will never abandon his policy about "the Holy Places." It has led to the commencement of a war which will not be quenched till he obtains possession of them, and is extinguished in the catastrophe awaiting his presumption.

His determination to invade the Holy Land and to take forcible possession of the Holy Places then in possession of the power that will have purchased them of the Constantinopolitan, will stir up its indignation greatly. Ezekiel tells us the name of the power and the position it assumes. His words are, "*Sheba and Dedan, and the merchants of Tarshish, with all the young lions thereof,* shall say unto thee, Art thou *come* to take a spoil? Hast thou gathered thy company to take a prey? to carry away silver and gold, to take away cattle and goods, to take a great spoil?" Let it be noted that the power does not say, "Art thou *gone* to take a spoil?" but, "Art thou *come* to do so?" If it were to say, "Art thou gone?" it would show that the power was beyond the limits of the Holy Land; but in saying, *Art thou come?* the conclusion is, that the Lion-power of Tarshish is in actual possession of the country.

These interrogatories put in a minatory form are the tidings out of the east and north that trouble him. They do not deter him, however, for Ezekiel relates that the invasion nevertheless ensues; and Daniel adds, with great fury for destruction. He rushes to meet his overthrow at the hand of God, who will thus demonstrate to all nations that no power injures Israel with impunity.

Sheba is south-southeast from Judea, by the Straits of Babelmandeb. It was one of the countries trading with Tyre in ancient times in "the chief of all spices, precious stones, and gold;" and is now preëminently connected with Tyre's

---

[1] Isai. vi. 13.

daughter, who has planted her standard on its soil at Aden, the Gibraltar of the Red Sea, and key of Egypt. Victoria may therefore be said to be the Queen of Sheba, and may possibly live (for she is young enough) to abdicate her throne, and to lay her crown and treasures at the feet of the "greater than Solomon," who will dispose of her and her affairs according to his will.

Dedan is another district of Arabia to the north-east of Sheba towards the Persian Gulf, and at present occupied by the Imam of Muscat. The men of Dedan are in the list given by Ezekiel of the traders in the Tyrian fairs. The Dedanim carried thither the ivory and ebony which they procured from "the many isles," or rather coasts, to the eastward, and "precious clothes for chariots." Thus Sheba and Dedan are those parts of Arabia which lay convenient to the ivory, gold, precious stones, and spice countries of Africa and India. Dedan has yet to come under the Lion-Power of the east and north.

As to Tarshish, there were two regions so called in the geography of the ancients. Jehoshaphat built ships at Eziongeber, a port of the Red Sea, that they might sail thence to Tarshish. Now, it will be seen by the map that they could only sail southward towards the Strait of Babelmandeb, from which they might then steer east, or north for India. As they did not sail by compass in those days, but coastwise, they would creep round the coast of Arabia and so make for Hindostan. The voyage occupied them three years. In the days of Solomon, the trade was shared between Israel and the Tyrians; for "he had at sea a navy of Tarshish with the navy of Hiram.; once in three years came the navy of Tarshish, bringing gold and silver, ivory, and apes, and peacocks." These products point to India as the eastern Tarshish—a country which has always conferred maritime ascendancy on the power which has possessed its trade and been its carrier to the nations.

But there was also a Tarshish to the north-west of Judea. This appears in the case of Jonah, who embarked at Joppa, now Jaffa, on the Mediterranean, "to flee into Tarshish from the presence of the Lord." He could only sail towards the west. Like the eastern Tarshish it was a country, not a city, whose "merchants" frequented the Tyrian fairs. Addressing Tyre, the prophet says, "Tarshish was thy merchant by reason of the multitude of all kinds of riches; with silver, iron, tin, and lead, they traded in thy fairs." These metals are preëminently the products of Britain, celebrated by the Phenicians as *Baratanac* or "the land of tin," as some interpret it. The merchandise of the northern Tarshish and of the eastern, identifies Britain in the north, and India in the east, with the two countries of that name.

But corroborative of this, I remark further that the Sheba and Tarshish power is represented as *a Merchant-power* in the words, "the Merchants of Tarshish shall say unto thee, O Gog." Having ascertained the geography of Tarshish, it is easy to answer the question, Who are signified by its merchants? This inquiry will admit of but one answer, namely, *The British East India Company of Merchants*, which is both the merchant and ruler of the elephant-tooth country of the east. But the association of "the young lions of Tarshish" with the "merchants of Tarshish," makes this still more obvious; for it represents *the peculiar constitution* of the Anglo-Indian government. It is well known that this government is a sovereignty of a mixed character, being neither purely merchant nor purely imperial. The Anglo-Canadian is purely imperial, no company of merchants having any share in its direction. But the Anglo-Indian government is constituted differently, the power having been founded by a chartered company of traders, and the British government afterwards admitted to a controlling influence in its Indian management. Now the imperial constituent of the power is represented by "*young lions;*" that is, the Lion is the symbol of the British power, which is therefore *the old lion;* while those who administer the power are *the young lions*. The lion-power is represented in the Anglo-Indian government by "the Board of Control,"

The merchants of Tarshish govern India under the control of the Lion-power—a constitution of things well represented on the company's shield of arms, whose quarterings are filled with young lions rampant, with a motto inscribed "*Auspicio Senatus Angliæ*. From these data, then, it may be fairly concluded, that the combined British and Indo-merchant power is the power of the latter days, raised up of God to antagonize the Russian power, so as by its policy and resistance to shape its course into the Valley of Decision, when, having laid all Europe prostrate, its insatiable ambition shall prompt it to seize upon Jerusalem and to grasp the sceptre of the east.

But the Lion-power of Britain has not not yet attained the full extent marked out for it by the finger of God. The annexation of Persia and Khush, or Khushistan, to the Gogian empire, will doubtless cause England to strengthen herself in Affghanistan, and possess herself of Dedan that she may command the entrance to the Persian Gulf, so as to prevent the King of the North from carrying war into the heart of India by land or sea. Possessing Persia and Mesopotamia, the apprehension of the dominion extending still further southward, perhaps to the very shores of the Red Sea, and so outflanking her by the Straits of Babelmandeb, will also be a powerful motive for the merchants of Tarshish and its young lions to take possession of all the coast from the Gulf of Persia to the Straits, and thence to Suez.

From the evidence, then, now before the reader, it is clear that the Tarshish antagonist to Gog is the British power, from which proceed the tidings that trouble the King of the North. At that time the Old World will be divided into *two great adverse confederacies*, of which Russia and Britain will be the powers in chief; the former having the lordship of the earth defined,* and the latter of the sea and its coast to a great extent. The British empire, not to mention its provinces which have no bearing upon the Gogian dominion, will then comprise the Indian Tarshish, the Muscat-Dedan, the Aden-Sheba, Edom, Moab, Ammon, Egypt, and Palestine; and perhaps all the islands of the Mediterranean, which will then vindicate its claim to its ancient name in the geography of Israel, "*The Sea of Tarshish.*"

The premises now before us also establish the position, that as Nebuchadnezzar's Image is representative of the Gogian empire in full manifestation, it is impossible in the nature of things that Britain can be one of the Ten Toes; and as the Toes of the Image represent the same powers as the Ten Horns of the Fourth Beast, and of the Dragon and Ten-horned apocalyptic Beasts, neither can she be included among the powers prefigured by those symbols.

29. THE LATTER DAYS.

The phrase *the latter days* occurs twice in the prophecy of Daniel, and therefore requires a word or two of explanation. The first place in which it is found is in chap. ii. 28, where Daniel tells Nebuchadnezzar that what he saw in his dream was a representation of "*what shall be in the latter days;*" and the other place is in chap. x. 14, where a messenger from God tells the prophet that he had come to make him understand "*what,*" said he, "*shall befall thy people* (Judah) *in the latter days,*" as represented in the vision of the 2300 evening-morning he had seen some years before. The occurrence of the phrase in these two places establishes a connection between the breaking of the image and the things pertaining to the Jews—in other words, between the fall of the Kingdom of Babylon and the setting up of the Kingdom of God.

It is important to the understanding of the prophecy that we should know the time referred to by the phrase. To ascertain this is easy. It may be known

*See p. 69.

whether they are past or future by a certain event which is to transpire in the time they indicate. The event is predicted by Hosea in these words: "The children of Israel shall abide many days without a king, and without a prince, and without a sacrifice, &c.; afterwards shall the children of Israel return, and seek Jehovah their God, and David their king; and shall fear Jehovah, and his goodness *in the latter days.*" Here is a long period indicated, termed "*many days,*" during which the Isrealites were to be without king, prince, or sacrifice. It is evident that that period is not yet ended, because they are still without those elements of their polity. *The latter days cannot therefore be in the past;* for the prophet says, "*afterward*" they shall *return* and seek David and Jehovah in the latter days. The latter days, then, are *after the ending of the many days,* and consequently still in the future.

The latter days are the latter years of the time of the end; and will be the most remarkable of any in the history of our post-diluvian world. They are styled in Daniel, "*a time of trouble such as never was since there was a nation to that same time.*" This is conceivable when we come to understand what the scriptures testify is then to be accomplished. The empire symbolized by the Image is to be broken to pieces, and the fragments ground to powder in the latter days; Gog is to come against the mountains of Israel in the latter days; the twelve tribes are to return to the Holy Land in the latter days; the Star that has arisen out of Jacob, and the sceptre out of Israel, "shall smite the princes of Moab, and destroy all the children of Sheth; and Israel shall do valiantly" in the latter days;[1] "a whirlwind of the Lord goes forth in fury, even a grievous whirlwind; it shall fall grievously on the head of the wicked. The anger of Jehovah shall not return, until he have executed, and have performed the thoughts of his heart; in the latter days, O Israel, ye shall consider it perfectly:"[2] the gathering of the peoples shall be to Shiloh in the latter days; and He shall rebuke strong nations afar off, and deliver Israel from the Assyrian in the latter days. In short, the latter days are "*the Hour of Judgment*" in which many of the dead are to arise, and the full measure of divine indignation shall be made manifest against "Christendom," which has so long triumphed over God's righteousness and truth.

30. THE "TIME OF TROUBLE."

POSITION OF THE RUSSIAN AND BRITISH FORCES AT THE ADVENT.

This terrible epoch precedes the *good time* celebrated traditionally in the ballads of the Gentiles. The termination of the King of the North's career is one of the great events of the crisis. Having been stirred up to fury by the defiance hurled against him by the Anglo-Tarshish power, and in consequence invaded the Holy Land, he will take up his position "*between the seas to the mountain, the glory of the holy;*" that is, between the Mediterranean and the Sea of Galilee, and from thence to the Holy City which he will invest with his forces. Thus he will be like a cloud preparing to cover the land marked out, being a distance of 70 miles from Jerusalem to the rear of his position, and about 35 miles from sea to sea. Within this area is included Jezreel and the plain of the ancient city Megiddo, celebrated in Jewish history for the great lamentation caused in Judah and Jerusalem because of the overthrow of their forces, and death of Josiah there at the hand of the Egyptians. As this was a notable national mourning, it is cited by Zechariah as an illustration of a future national lamentation at the time when "all nations shall come against Jerusalem,"[3] especially as they will overspread the field of Josiah's disaster. The whole area that will be occupied by the king of the north is represented in the Apocalypse by this celebrated section of it; and styled ARMAGEDDON, or *The Mountain of Megiddo.*

(1) Numb. xxiv. 14–19.   (2) Jer. xxiii. 19, 20; xxx. 19–24.   (3) Zech. xii. 9, 11.

On this area Daniel says, "*the king of the North shall plant the tents of his camp.*" He will then be at the head of the armies of all the nations of the Gogian dominion gathered against Jerusalem to battle, as Zechariah and other prophets have foretold. Well garrisoned and defended as the Holy City no doubt will be by the Anglo-Tarshish power and the Jews, the city will nevertheless be taken, but not destroyed; though great calamities will be inflicted upon the inhabitants. Jerusalem being taken, there is reason to believe that the war will be continued on the other side of the Jordan in that part of Ammon which does not escape out of the hand of the King of the North. This will extend the seat of the war to *Eastern* Idumea or Edom in the region of Bozrah; while *South* Edom, Moab, and the major part of Ammon escape its ravages. This will be the position of the two armies; Gog's extending from Egypt to Mount Carmel and the Sea of Tiberias northward; and from the Mediterranean to the Dead Sea; and from Carmel across the Jordan to Bozrah eastward: while the Anglo-Tarshish forces, cut off from the Mediterranean and their western fleet, will face the enemy in the northern part of Ammon, their communication with the ocean being maintained by the Red Sea.

This being the final position of the hostile armies, the reader will see the force of Isaiah's inquiry of the blood-stained traveller, "*Who is this that cometh from* Edom *with dyed garments from* Bozrah? *this that is glorious in his apparel, travelling in the greatness of his strength?*" These two armies contending against each other for the possession of Jehovah's Land are therefore Jehovah's enemies. In holding South Edom, the capital of which was Seir; Moab, and the major part of Ammon, &c., to Khushistan, Anglo-Tarshish will occupy a part of the territory covenanted to Abraham and Christ; while Gog at the same time holds the rest: to say nothing of their wickedness which is great, they are, because of this appropriation of the land, the enemies of Jehovah and his King; as it is written, "Edom shall be a possession, Seir also shall be a possession for his enemies."

Edom then may be styled the general quarters of the two armies; and therefore when Jehovah goes forth to fight them "as when he fought in the day of battle" in old time, he strikes the first blow at Bozrah. And a terrible blow it will be, as may be conceived from the answer to another question by the same prophet, saying, "Wherefore art thou red in thine apparel, and thy garments like him that treadeth in the winefat?" "I have trodden," says the traveller, "*the winepress* alone; and of the people there was none with me: for I will tread them in my anger, and trample them in my fury; and their blood shall be sprinkled upon my garments, and I will stain all my raiment: for the Day of Vengeance is in my heart, and the year of my redeemed is come. And I looked, and there was none to help; and I wondered that there was none to uphold; therefore mine own arm brought salvation to me; and my fury it upheld me. And I will tread down the people in mine anger, and make them drunk in my fury, and I will bring down their strength to the earth."[1]

From this we learn that when Isaiah sees him coming towards Jerusalem a blow had been struck, and that others remained to be inflicted; and that the Jews had afforded no coöperation. But who was this traveller from a far country whose appearance is attended with such sudden destruction? He answers the question by saying, "I that speak in righteousness, mighty to save:" or, as it is apocalyptically expressed, "The Faithful and True One, who in righteousness doth judge and make war: clothed with a vesture dipped in blood, whose name is called the Word of God."[2] Daniel styles him, "Michael the Great Commander, who standeth for Judah;" also "the Commander of commanders," which is equivalent to "King of kings, and Lord of lords." Hosea calls him Jezreel. Ezekiel terms him Adonai and the imperial forces which serve with the Company's troops in the Indian army.

---

(1) Isai. lxiii. 1-6. (2) Rev. xix. 11-13.

Jehovah; Isaiah, "the Name of Jehovah coming from far, burning with his anger;" and Paul, the Lord Jesus revealed from heaven, taking vengeance, consuming and destroying with the brightness of his coming.

The means by which in the absence of all coöperation his own arm brings salvation are terrific. The following testimonies will exhibit them : "The Lord shall cause the glory of his voice to be heard, and shall show the lighting down of his arm with the indignation of his anger, and with the flame of a devouring fire, with scattering, and tempest, and hailstones; for through the voice of the Lord shall the Assyrian be beaten down which smote with a rod. For Tophet is ordained of old; yea, for THE KING it is prepared; He hath made it deep and large: the pile thereof is fire, and much wood; the breath of Jehovah, like a stream of brimstone, doth kindle it."[1]

"When the Lord shall stretch out his hand, both he that helpeth shall fall, and he that is holpen shall fall down, and they all shall fall together. For thus hath the Lord spoken unto me, Like as the lion and the young lion roaring on his prey, when a multitude of shepherds is called forth against him, he will not be afraid of their voice, nor abase himself for the multitude of them: so shall Jehovah of armies come down to fight for Mount Zion, and for the hill thereof. As birds flying, so will Jehovah of armies defend Jerusalem; defending also he will deliver it; and passing over he will preserve it. In that day every man shall cast away his idols of silver and of gold. Then shall the Assyrian fall with the sword, . . . and his princes shall be afraid of THE ENSIGN, saith Jehovah, whose fire is in Zion, and his furnace in Jerusalem."[2]

And again, "Come near, ye nations, to hear; and hearken, ye people; let the earth hear, and all that is therein; the world, and all things that come forth of it; For the indignation of Jehovah is upon all nations, and his fury upon all their armies: he utterly destroys them, he hath delivered them to the slaughter. Their slain also shall be cast out, and their stench shall come up out of their carcasses, and the mountains shall be melted with their blood. And all the host of heaven shall be dissolved, and the heavens shall be rolled together as a scroll: and all their armies shall fall down, as the leaf falleth off from the vine, and as a falling from the fig tree. For my sword shall be bathed in heaven; behold it shall come down upon Edom, and upon the people of my curse, to judgment. The sword of Jehovah is filled with blood, it is made fat with fatness, and with the blood of lambs and goats, with the fat of the kidneys of rams; for Jehovah hath a sacrifice in Bozrah, and a great slaughter in the land of Edom. And *the Unicorns* (one of the symbols of Britain) shall come down with them, and the bullocks with the bulls; and their land shall be soaked with blood, and their dust made fat with fatness. For it is the Day of Jehovah's vengeance, the year of recompenses for the controversy of Zion."[3]

Furthermore, "I will call for a sword against Gog throughout all my mountains, saith Adonai Jehovah: every man's sword shall be against his brother. And I will plead against him with pestilence and with blood; and I will rain upon him, and upon his bands, and upon the many people that are with him, an overflowing rain, and great hailstones, fire, and brimstone. Speak unto every feathered fowl, and to every beast of the field, saying, Assemble yourselves, and come, gather yourselves on every side to my sacrifice that I do slaughter for you, a great sacrifice upon the mountains of Israel, that ye may eat flesh, and drink blood. Ye shall eat the flesh of the mighty, and drink the blood of the princes of the earth; and ye shall eat fat till ye be full, and drink blood till ye be drunken, of my sacrifice which I have slaughtered for you. Thus shall ye be filled at my table with horses and charioteers, with mighty men, and with all men of

---

(1) Isai. xxx. 30–33.   (2) Isai. xxxi. 3–9.   (3) Isai. xxxiv. 1–8.

war, saith the Lord God. And I will set my glory among the nations, and all the nations shall see my judgment that I have executed, and my hand that I have laid upon them. So the house of Israel shall know that I am Jehovah their God from that day and forward. And the nations shall know that the house of Israel went into captivity for their iniquity; because they trespassed against me, therefore I hid my face from them, and gave them into the hands of their enemies; so fell they all by the sword."[1]

"In the valley of Jehoshaphat will I sit to judge all the nations round about:"[2] "and I will execute vengeance in anger and fury upon them, such as they have not heard."[3] "In that day, saith Jehovah, I will smite every horse with consternation, and his rider with madness."[4] "Their flesh shall consume away while they stand upon their feet, and their eyes shall consume away in their orbits, and their tongue shall consume away in their mouth. And a great tumult from Jehovah shall be among them; and they shall lay hold every one on the hand of his neighbor, and his hand shall rise up against the hand of his neighbor."[5]

Thus will the Image be smitten, the Little Horn of the Goat broken without help, and the King of the North come to his end with none to help him—a catastrophe in which the struggle now beginning among the nations of the Old World will be sure to end.

31. THE DELIVERANCE OF ISRAEL OUT OF THE HAND OF THEIR ENEMIES.

"At that time thy people, Daniel, shall be delivered, every one that shall be found written in the book.

The name *Israel* deserves our attention briefly in speaking of their deliverance. Israel signifies *a Prince of God*. It was the name conferred on the grandson of Abraham, who was called Jacob, or *supplanter,* by his parents, in allusion to his posterity, who, though the descendants of the younger brother, should have the lordship over Edom, the country of Esau the elder.

When this new and divinely-bestowed name was confirmed to Jacob at Bethel, in the Holy Land, the messenger of the God of Abraham said to him, "Thy name is Jacob; thy name shall not be called any more Jacob, but *Israel* shall be thy name: and he called his name Israel. And God said unto him, *A nation* and *a company of nations* shall be of thee, and *kings* shall come out of thy loins; and the *land* which I gave Abraham and Isaac, to *thee* will I give it, and to *thy Seed* after thee will I give the land."[6] Jacob, now called Israel, as Abraham and Isaac had before him, died without realizing any of these promised blessings; nevertheless in the terminus of his mortal career he still looked for the enjoyment of them. *An Israelitish Royalty in the land of Canaan, when it should be in his own possession and in that of his Seed*, had been promised him of God; and he believed it with full assurance of hope, "being fully persuaded that what he had promised, he was able also to perform." The unpropitious circumstances by which he was surrounded in the Egyptian province of Goshen did not dim the brightness of his expectation for a moment. On his dying-bed by his twelve sons surrounded, he directed their attention to the events that should happen to their posterity at a period far remote, באחרית הימים, *bĕăchărith hyyămim,* "in the uttermost part of the days," the prophetic formula for *the latter days.* He predicted that Levi's posterity should be "divided in Jacob, and scattered in Israel," because "in their anger they slew a man," (that is, Messiah.) But in Judah he saw "*the Seed*" who should as king of the nation rule the land; therefore he said, "Judah, thou art he whom thy brethren shall praise: *thy hand shall be in the neck of thine enemies;* thy father's children shall bow down before thee. Judah is a lion's

---

(1) Ezek. xxxviii. 21, 22; xxxix. 17–23.   (2) Joel iii. 12.   (3) Micah v. 15.
(4) Zech. xii. 4.   (5) Zech. xiv. 12.   (6) Gen. xxxv. 10–12.

whelp: *from the prey*, my son, thou art gone up: he stooped down, he couched as a lion, and as an old lion; who shall rouse him up? The *sceptre* shall not depart from Judah, nor a Lawgiver from between his feet, until rest shall come, and to him (the Lawgiver) the peoples shall gather. Binding his foal unto the vine, and his ass's colt unto the choice vine; he washed his garments in wine, and his clothes in the blood of grapes: his eyes (fountains) shall be red with wine, and his teeth (rocks) white with milk."

But while he saw the Royalty in conquering Judah, he beheld in the life of his son Joseph a striking illustration of Him who should be the strength and glory of their nation; for as Joseph was sold by his brethren, and a long time separate from them, such also should be the fate of him upon whose head the crown of Joseph's royalty should rest, before he should obtain the kingdom in the latter days. As Jacob predicted, "the archers have sorely grieved, shot at, and hated the posterity of Joseph:" yet "his bow abides in strength," though long unstrung: but when the King of the North shall be broken, "the arms of Joseph's hands shall be made strong by the hands of the Mighty One of Jacob; proceeding forth from whom is the Shepherd, the Stone of Israel;" and therefore Son of God as well as Judah's son.

The name *Israel* by inheritance has descended to this Royal Nation, to which all the good things, called "*the goodness of Jehovah*," foreshadowed in their law, and predicted by their prophets, belong. "*To Israel*," says Paul, "*pertain the adoption, and the glory, and the covenants, and the giving of the law, and the service, and the promises.*"[1] Hence, it is manifest, that one of another nation must become the subject of that "*adoption*," before he can become an heir of those "*covenants*" and "*promises*." He must therefore put off his Gentilism, and become an adopted citizen of Israel's Commonwealth; which places him upon an equal footing with the most favored of the nation.

But, "they are not all Israel who are of Israel: neither because they are the seed of Abraham, are they all children." The natural descendants of Abraham, Isaac, and Jacob, numerous as the sand of the sea, who have gone down to the grave, are not the Israel—*the generations of the nation*—that shall inhabit the Holy Land when Abraham, Isaac, Jacob, David, Christ, their Seed, and *all in him*, shall possess it for ever. It is only "*a remnant shall be saved*" of them—a remnant "who walked in the steps of that faith of their father Abraham which he had when yet uncircumcised." This is also true of all Israelites according to the flesh, living contemporary with the overthrow of the king of the north—"a remnant will be saved;" all of them that "abide not in unbelief shall be grafted in: for God is able to graft them in again;" *and only He*. This latter-day remnant will be saved, however, in a different sense from that in which the remnant in the grave will experience salvation. These "awake to everlasting life" to possess the kingdom and glory for ever; whereas the others continuing subject to death individually are saved nationally from their down-trodden condition among the nations; and established as an independent and powerful nation in the Holy Land, under the sceptre of Jacob's Star, whose dominion shall be acknowledged throughout the earth. Their salvation is a restoration to Canaan, and a national regeneration to newness of intellectual, moral, civil, and religious life.

All Gentiles who believe the good message concerning this kingdom and obey it, before "Michael the great prince" stands up to overthrow the King of the North, by that *obedience of faith* become Israelites in the higher sense. Whether dead or living, they are numbered with the remnant of the obedient "who sleep in the dust of the earth." Believing the promises to Israel, and *therefore* being baptized, gives an Israelite, or one of another nation, introduction into Christ; "in

---

(1) Rom. ix. 4.

whom being they are circumcised with the circumcision made without hands in putting off the body of the sins of the flesh by the circumcision of Christ." [1] Such are then Israelites in a sense in which the natural descendants of Abraham are not; still these do not cease to be Israelites in an inferior sense, and the objects of deliverance from existing national degradation.

When Michael the great prince stands up for the overthrow of Israel's enemies, he finds them and Israel shut up in unbelief—the Gentiles *without faith in the kingdom;* and the Jews *without faith in its king;* both conditions being equally fatal to a participation with Christ in the glory, honor, incorruptibility, and life, which are the special attributes of the princes of regenerated Israel. He will also find a multitude of Jews in the Holy Land as faithless in Jesus as the generation that crucified him; for it is to make a spoil of these that Gog invades the land.[2] The calamities of war, however, greatly reduce their numbers. Whatever the whole number may be, it is diminished two thirds. "In all the land, saith Jehovah, two parts therein shall be cut off and die; but the third shall be left therein. And I will bring the third part through the fire, and will refine them as silver is refined, and will try them as gold is tried: they shall call on my name, and I will hear them: I will say, It is my people: and they shall say, Jehovah is my God."[3]

With this third part as *a nucleus* the kingdom of God begins under Michael and his associates. It is then as a grain of mustard-seed, but destined to become a great tree whose branches shall overshadow the earth. The third part refined are they of Israel belonging to the tents of Judah, of whom it is written, "Jehovah shall save the tents of Judah first," and then Jerusalem, as appears from the reason given, "that the glory of the house of David, and the glory of the inhabitants of Jerusalem, do not magnify themselves against Judah." It is this third part that will "look upon Him whom they have pierced, and shall mourn for him, as one mourneth for his only son, and shall be in bitterness for him, as one that is in bitterness for his first-born." They will find that Michael, the Deliverer, is Jehovah the Powerful (*Jesus* in Greek) whom their fathers nailed to the accursed tree; for, "One shall say unto Him, What are these wounds in thine hand? Then he shall answer, Those with which I was wounded in the house of my friends!"

But, while this third part is delivered consequent on the overthrow of the Gentile armies throughout the land, the deliverance of the nation still remains to be effected. Having finished the prediction of Gog's destruction, by which the Holy is avenged, Jehovah proceeds to say, "*Now* will I bring again the captivity of Jacob, and have mercy upon *the whole house of Israel,* and will be jealous for my holy name." Hence, the order of events is, *first,* the avenging of the holy land in the overthrow of the Gentile armies upon the mountains of Israel; *secondly,* the saving of the tents of Judah; *thirdly,* the deliverance of Jerusalem; *fourthly,* the bringing of the whole house of Israel not in the land at the saving of Judah's tents into the Wilderness of the People to bear their shame there for forty years; and *fifthly,* the bringing of them from thence, "after they have borne their shame," into the land of Israel; and making them one nation with Judah under the New Covenant, by which Jehovah's Servant, David II., becomes their High Priest and King for *a season and a time.* The whole house of Israel thus united under One Head into one nation and kingdom, for the first time since the revolt of the Ten Tribes from the house of David in the third year of Solomon's successor, is that kingdom represented by THE STONE in Nebuchadnezzar's dream, of which it is written, "In the days of these kings (of Gog's confederacy) the God of heaven shall set up a kingdom which shall never perish; and a dominion that shall not be left to another people. It shall grind to powder and bring to an end all these kingdoms; and itself shall stand for ever." Now when this work is perfected, it is manifest that

---

(1) Col. ii. 11   (2) Ezek. xxxviii. 8.   (3) Zech. xiii. 8, 9.

Israel will be delivered from all their enemies, and the power of the holy people no longer scattered. Jehovah says, that not one of them shall be left in their enemies' lands, such a thorough gleaning will he make of them from among the nations. This grafting in again of Israel into their own olive tree is the horizon that bounds the view of Daniel's telescope. There are no events beyond it revealed in his prophecy. It is the terminus of all his visions—the vanishing point upon which all his groups of symbols terminate: so that in the seventh verse of the last chapter it is written, that the revealing angel, in answer to the question, "*How long to the end of these wonders?*" held up his hands to heaven, and "sware by Him that liveth for ever that it shall be for *a time, times, and an half;* and when he shall have accomplished to scatter the power of the holy people, all these wonders shall be finished."

With these premises before us it will not be difficult to answer the inquiry, Who are Daniel's people, and their children, for whom Michael standeth up? They are the righteous dead of Israel, both native-born and adopted; *secondly*, the contemporary living believers who have obeyed the gospel of the kingdom; and *thirdly*, Judah's third part, and the rising generation of the rest of Israel disciplined in the Wilderness of the People subsequently to the fall of Gog on Jehovah's mountains. These all in the aggregate constitute the Saints, and the People of the Saints, for whose deliverance Michael stands up in the time of trouble. Abel and Noah; Abraham, Isaac and Jacob; Moses and all the prophets; the apostles and an innumerable company redeemed from among men, will then awake from their long sleep to sing the praises of Him who will have raised them to reign with him upon the earth: while some others who would not that he should rule Jehovah's people, and govern the nations, will leave the dust to wail and gnash their teeth in shame and contempt among the papal or devil-nations of the west. There beyond the great gulf in exile from the Holy Land, they will be tormented among the worshippers of the Beast and his Image with fire and brimstone in the presence of the holy angels, and in the presence of the Lamb.

The phrase in Daniel, "Every one that is found written in the book," has a two-fold signification; the first in regard to the righteous, both alive and dead; and the second, to Judah's third part. Malachi affords us the interpretation in the first sense, and Isaiah in the last. Thus: "They that feared Jehovah spake often one to another; and Jehovah hearkened, and heard it; and *a book of remembrance was written before him* for them that feared Jehovah, and that thought upon his name. And they shall be mine, saith Jehovah of armies, in that day when I make up my jewels"[1]—the day when Michael stands up for them.

Speaking of the day in which the Lord alone shall be exalted, Isaiah says: "In that day shall the Branch of Jehovah (Judah) be beautiful and glorious; and the fruit of the land excellent and comely for them that are escaped of Israel. And it shall be that he that is left in Zion, and he that remaineth in Jerusalem, shall be called holy, even *every one that is written among the living in Jerusalem*, when the Lord shall have washed away the filth of the daughters of Zion, and shall have purged the blood of Jerusalem from the midst thereof by the spirit of judgment, and by the spirit of burning."[2] These will be delivered by destroying the enemy out of the Holy City; the others, by resurrection from the dead; for, "Many of them that sleep in the dust of the earth shall awake to everlasting life—and they that be wise shall shine as the brightness of the firmament; and they that turn many to righteousness as the stars in the age and ever."

32. RESURRECTION TO JUDGMENT IN THE WAR OF GOD ALMIGHTY.

But, while some are to arise to the life of the Age, others are to awake from the

---

(1) Mal. iii. 16; Exod. xxxii. 32; Rev. xxi. 27.   (2) Isai. iv. 2–4.

dust of the earth "to the reproaches and abhorrence of the age." This will be a new element in the trouble of this disastrous time. This class of Jews are doubtless those whom Jesus referred to in reproducing the words of Daniel, saying, "The hour is coming in the which all that are in the graves shall hear the voice of the Son of Man (or Michael) and shall come forth; they that have done good things unto a resurrection of life; and they that have done evil things unto a resurrection of judgment." In these words Christ shows that resurrection precedes rewards and punishments. He speaks of Daniel's "*many*" as the *all in the graves*; in certain particular graves; from which some will come forth to take forcible possession of the kingdom of Babylon; and, having wrested it from its Gentile rulers, to reign over its populations with Christ for a season and time; while others come forth to participate subjectively in the judgment to be executed upon the nations, peoples, and languages subject to the fourth beast which is to be destroyed by the burning flame. Of the latter class are they to whom Jesus said, "There shall be weeping and gnashing of teeth when ye shall see Abraham, Isaac, and Jacob, and all the prophets in the kingdom of God, and you yourselves cast out." This casting out is exile from the Holy Land to the countries then still in the possession of the powers, indicated as "the Beast, the False Prophet, and the kings of the earth," and styled by Christ, "*the Devil and his Angels.*"[1] This region of the kingdom of Babylon is separated from the Holy Land by a great gulf, called the Mediterranean, which being subject to Michael's power, those who would repass into Judea will not be able.[2] The apocalyptic name of this judicial region, or country where judgment is to be executed by the saints,[3] is "*a lake of fire burning with brimstone.*"[4] With the goat-nations of this region the resurrected exiles will be commingled, that they may there "drink of the wine of the wrath of God, which is poured out without mixture into the cup of his indignation; and be tormented with fire and brimstone in the presence of the holy messengers, and in the presence of the Lamb."[5] This tormenting, as I have hinted already, is "the war of the great day of God Almighty,"[6] in which Christ and his associates, as the commanders of the Twelve Tribes, are engaged for the destruction of the kingdom of men. The *material* of the war is symbolized by "fire and brimstone;" and, being brought to bear upon the objects of divine indignation by the people of the holy ones as the soldiery of Christ and his associates in command, the battle-torment is very fitly represented as being inflicted "in the presence of the holy messengers and in the presence of the Lamb." The saints are styled οἱ ἅγιοι αγγελοι, *hoi hagioi angeloi*, "the holy angels," or messengers, because they are sent by the Ancient of Days to destroy the fourth beast, or Latin and Greek powers of Babylon. This is the judgment into which resurrection introduces those "who know not God and *obey not the gospel* of Jesus Christ." Exiles among human devils and their princes, they are even there the objects of reproaches and abhorrence. Whether their miserable existence will be prolonged after the war of God Almighty against the Powers of the Gentiles shall have ceased, there is no testimony in Daniel to determine. The words of Jesus would lead one to conclude that it is not; for he says, concerning them, "Those mine enemies who would not that I should reign over them, bring hither, and slay them before me;"[7] or, apocalyptically, "in the presence of me, the Lamb." When this sentence is executed upon them, death lays hold of them *a second time*, and they "reap corruption" as the threatened consequence of "sowing to the flesh." Hence, not having their names written in the Book of Life, they are expelled from Paradise, "that they might not eat of the Tree of Life and live for ever." Death is therefore the eternal consummation that awaits them—Death, consequent upon their "having

(1) Mat. xxv. 41. (2) Luke xvi. 26. (3) Ps. cxlix. 5–9. (4) Rev. xix. 20.
(5) Rev. xiv. 10. (6) Rev. xvi. 14. (7) Luke xix. 27.

their part in the lake which burneth with fire and brimstone: *which is the Second Death*."[1] Thus, "the wages of sin is death; but the gracious *gift* of God is everlasting life through Jesus Christ the Lord."

A word of explanation may be deemed necessary concerning the phrase "*human devils and their princes*," among whom I have said the resurrected enemies of Jesus are to be objects of abhorrence and reproach in the hour of judgment. In the heraldry of the Bible the subjects of dominions are designated and distinguished by the symbols or emblems which represent the power. Thus, the Goat is representative of Greece; therefore the Greeks and their princes are styled *goats*; and the Lion, of Anglo-Tarshish; therefore the British are termed "the young lions thereof." Now, the confederacy of Gentile powers under the Autocrat of all the Russias in the latter days, is not only symbolized by Nebuchadnezzar's Image, and called *Gōg*; but it is also represented by "THE DRAGON," which is to be "bound for a thousand years," by the destruction of the fourth beast, and the taking away the dominion of the Lion-Man, the Bear, and the Leopard, for a season and time: the subjects therefore of the Dragon-dominion are *Dragons*. The dragon was the symbol selected by the Romans to represent their imperiality. But the Spirit of God did not deem it sufficiently expressive of the character of the power, which in the time of trouble is to be *an imperial organization of sin*, specially manifested as *the Adversary* of Michael, his associates, and Israel their people. The Sin-Imperiality, having its root in the serpent-excited rebellion of the parents of our race against God, is styled "*that old Serpent;*" while Michael and his party, at the epoch of the binding, antagonize it as the Woman and her Seed. Hence, to express the great wickedness of the Dragon-power, and its "*enmity*" to all pertaining to the Holy Land, it is "surnamed Diabolos and Satanas," rendered in the common version "the Devil and Satan;" which is not a translation, but a transfer of the untranslated words into an English connection. The sentence in which they occur is, ὁ οφις ὁ αρχαιος ὁς ἐστι διαβολος και σατανας. *ho ophis ho archaios, hos esti diabolos kai sutanas;* and which in plain English signifies, "*The old serpent, who is that causing to fall and an adversary.*" This will have ever been characteristic of all the administrations of the Kingdom of Babylon from Nebuchadnezzar to the last of the czars, popes, emperors, and kings of the Dragon-confederacy. These are the princes, or "angels" of the Devil-and-Satan power; hence the phrase "*Devil and his angels*," whose power is to be destroyed by the fiery stream issuing forth from the Ancient of Days; that is, by the consuming and destructive energy of Michael and his hosts. The power, then, being commonly styled "the Devil" in the English scriptures, all who are subject to its dominion, not being of the household of faith, are "human devils and their princes." Their imperial chief is the head of the serpent-power, which is to be so bruised and crippled that it shall be chieftainless for a thousand years.

33. "THE WISE."
"*The wise shall understand.*"

The war of God Almighty, which begins subsequently to the resurrection of the holy ones, does not intermit, till all the Kingdoms of imperial Babylon become theirs. As conquerors of the powers that overcame them in the days of their flesh, the praises of emancipated nations sound the fame of Israel to the ends of the earth. As a nation they become mighty and glorious above all. But if the nation be so great, what may not be expected of those who shall have led the tribes of Jacob to victory and renown, and under the generalship of their commander-in-chief shall have brought the blessings of Abraham upon the world? Daniel anticipates this inquiry by saying, "And they that be *wise* shall shine as the brightness of the firmament; and they that turn many to righteousness as the

---
(1) Rev. xxi. 8.

stars for the age and ever." Speaking of the same period Jesus, also says, "Then shall *the righteous* shine forth as the sun in the Kingdom of their Father." It is clear, then, that when Daniel's prediction shall come to pass, the Kingdom will have been established—the work of setting it up will have been finished; and that consequently, Israel will have been grafted into their own olive, and therefore be not only "the people of the holy ones," but "the holy people;" a distinction not without a difference. The only place in the original of Daniel where Israel is styled "the holy people," is in the seventh verse of the last chapter, where the time is announced at the end of which their power shall be no more in the scattered condition it now is; but when he predicted their destruction by the Little Horn and the taking away of the evening and morning sacrifice, in the eighth chapter and twenty-fourth verse, he styled them "the people of the holy ones," but very far from being a holy people. Well, at that time, when the people of the holy ones are a holy people; that is, at the end of the time, times, and the half of a time, or 1260 years, the wise shall shine in the Kingdom of the God of heaven. But then, *Who are the wise?*

This is a very important question. It is truly a vital question to every one that reads it. As the inquiry is suggested by Daniel, would it not be proper to let him suggest the answer? This I think is expedient; certainly preferable to the suggestion emanating from myself. Let us, then, hear what he testifies. He tells us that the revealing angel said to him at the end of his discourse, " Go thou thy way, Daniel," or desist from further inquiries, in reply to a question he put for information, but which was not granted. "I heard," said he, "but I understood not: then said I, O my Lord, *when the end of these?"* that is, of the time, times, and a half?—מה אחרית אלה, *mā ăchărith aileh*. He was told the reason why he could not obtain the information sought; that it was "because the words were closed up and sealed *till the time of the end;*" which was tantamount to saying that when the time of the end should arrive, the time-words would be no longer closed up and sealed; that is, they would speak or become intelligible; for in that time many should run to and fro, and knowledge should be increased. On a previous page I have shown that "the time of the end" has been present with us for several years; during which many have been running to and fro, to the increase of knowledge considerably. As a result of this Daniel was informed, in effect, that his question would then be solved, and besides was given to know who should not, and who should understand it. "*None of the* רשעים *rĕshāim, unjust* shall understand; but *the wise shall understand.*" The word reshaim signifies *unjustified persons* as opposed to צדיקים tzaddikim, *justified persons*, who are "the wise." This criticism accords with the words of Jesus, who substitutes the phrase the *tzaddikim* or righteous, for "the wise," in the text already quoted; and very properly, for none can become *righteous* who are not circumspect of mind, intelligent, or carefully considerate of the divine testimony, which is the meaning of משכילים, *măskilim*, translated *wise*.

But, if the wise are to be determined by those who can answer the question, "*When the end of the time, times, and a half?"* where shall they be found? Some ten years ago in these United States, we had a multitude of *Reshaim*, who claimed to be *Maskilim* upon the ground that they could answer the question! They published far and wide that the end would be in 1843! But time has proved that they were *Reshaim*, and not *Maskilim;* for "*none of them understood.*" Wisdom, however, hath her beginning in the fear of the Lord, which is precisely the alpha with which they omitted to commence their studies. "Children, I will *teach* you the fear of the Lord." It is a something to be taught, studied, and acquired. "The fear of the Lord is *the instruction* of wisdom;" that *way of acceptance with God* which the Spirit of wisdom teaches in the holy scriptures. In the days of his flesh, Jesus was "*of quick understanding* in the fear of the Lord;" and so are they who besides him are "taught of God;" and it is only they who are thus taught that are recognized as righteous; for of these is it written, "they shall be all taught of God."[1] But, *how doth God teach men his fear?* In the days of the apostles he taught them through the scriptures of the prophets, and the oral instructions of the apostles; but since their time, *by the scriptures of the prophets and apostles only:* for an apostle says, "*The scriptures are able to make wise to salvation* through faith which is in Christ Jesus." And again, he says, "All scripture given by inspiration of God is profitable for teaching, for conviction, for correction, for instruction in righteousness: that the man of God may be perfect, thoroughly furnished unto all good works." Here then is God's agency for teaching men his wisdom. And what more do men need than to be made wise to salvation, instructed in righteousness, perfected, and thoroughly furnished for the manifestation of good works? They must study it for themselves, thankfully availing themselves of all the help they can obtain from others, who have been taught of God before them. "If any man consent not to the wholesome words of our Lord Jesus, and to the teaching which is according to godliness, he is proud, knowing nothing." Now, he preached the gospel of the kingdom, and commanded all who believed it to be immersed. He prescribed baptism to no one else; because no one could be benefited by it who was not first a divinely instructed believer of the Kingdom's gospel. Those who have obeyed this gospel are the *Tzaddikim*, or justified; those who have not obeyed it are the *Reshaim*, or unjustified. These are not taught of God; their fear of him, such as it is, is taught them by the precepts of men. The class is very large, and composed of innumerable orders, which, however diversified, have one common characteristic—they are "contentious, and obey not the truth;" they "stumble at the word, being disobedient."[2] None of these shall understand. This is the divine sentence against them, and accounts for the failure of the many learned writers upon prophecy, to say nothing of the unlearned, in the enterprise of reading correctly the past and future of the world by the light of the prophetic word: most of them lived too soon, and all of them were ignorant of the gospel; so that being *Reshaim*, with all their learning they could only demonstrate each other's foolishness, without any of them succeeding in pointing out the truth.

The *wise*, then, of the time of the end are those who believe "the things concerning the kingdom of God, and the name of Jesus Christ;" and have *therefore* been "immersed into the name of the Father, and of the Son, and of the Holy Spirit."[3] He who understands these things has laid the foundation of intelligence in the things which Daniel heard, but understood not. Being wise, he shall understand them if he give heed thereto. This is the encouragement given; and to help them in the endeavor is the purpose of this book; that they may not be taken at unawares by the consummation that approaches rapidly.

34. THE TIMES OF THE KINGDOM OF BABYLON AND OF JUDAH.

The idea prominently sustained throughout the book of Daniel is, as we have seen, *one dominion under divers administrations*, styled the kingdom of men, or of Babylon, as opposed to the kingdom of Judah, which is God's. Both these kingdoms have their times, or periods, during which their reigns are unrivalled. The two kingdoms, however, being essentially hostile and destructive of one another, it so happens that when one reigns prosperously, the other must be in adversity, or extinct. This being the case, it is obvious that the prosperity of the two kingdoms must pertain to different and successive ages, and that the practising

---

(1) John vi. 44, 45.   (2) Rom. ii. 8; 1 Pet. ii. 8.   (3) Acts viii. 12; Mat. xxviii. 19.

and prospering of the one is at the expense of the others. Now this is a truth that is self-evident to all acquainted with the history of Judah and the Gentiles, or other nations. From the celebrated Passover in the eighteenth of Josiah's reign to the present time, has been a period of calamity for the Jews; and from the first of Nebuchadnezzar's, which was seventeen years after, to the same epoch, a period of ascendancy and treading down for the Babylonian kingdom of men. During this long interval of about 2463 years, the stump of the Babylonish Tree, "banded with iron and brass," has continued with its roots in the earth. But when its time shall have passed over it, "the stump of its roots" will be removed; and the times of the reign of the kingdom of God will begin. These continue without change for a thousand years, at the end of which perfection being attained, the constitution of the kingdom will be altered to meet the improved condition of the world. Thenceforth, all things will be permanent, and generations will cease to come and go. The unrighteous will have been exterminated; and the earth will be inhabited by immortals only, who will have attained to immortality upon the condition of *believing heartily what God has promised and taught in his word prophetically and apostolically ministered; and of doing what he there requires to be done.* A kingdom having God the Invisible in all for its king; the Anointed One and his brethren for its princes; and the redeemed from among Israel and the nations during the previous thousand years for its nation of immortals, will be our globe's "*New Heavens and Earth*" that shall never wax old nor vanish away. Its times, therefore, will be interminable, an idea expressed by the phrase "the ages of the ages."

But the times of the kingdom of Babylon cannot be calculated without reference to the times of Judah's adversity. The reason of this is, that when these end, Israel's Commander in Chief and his associates at the head of the tribes begin the work of Babylon's destruction, which they accomplish in the time allotted for the restoration of the kingdom again to Israel. Hence there is a parallelism between Babylon and Judah's times that must not be lost sight of; for Babylon is only a subject of prophecy so far as it is in opposition to the things of the kingdom of God.

Now, the whole number of the times of the continuance of the kingdom of Babylon is *seven times;* and the whole number of the times at the end of which Judah's subjection to it shall cease, is also seven. The truth of this in relation to Babylon appears from *the sign* recorded in the fourth chapter of Daniel. There Babylon's dominion is represented by a tree so lofty that it was seen from the end of the earth. But it was revealed to Nebuchadnezzar by what happened to the tree and to himself, that the dominion should not always continue in his family and the city he so proudly boasted of. He was, however, instructed by his seven years' expulsion from the throne, and the kingdom, nevertheless, being assured to him, that though Babylon should cease to be the throne of the dominion, the Babylonish kingdom would exist in the earth for the period signified by the seven times; when it would become apparent to all the nations of the dominion, that "the Heavens do rule."

The *seven times* during which Nebuchadnezzar herded with the beasts were the *sign-period* significative of a longer period than itself; yet containing within itself the elements of the calculation. "*A day for a year*" is a rule to which all prophetic times are reducible. In seven times, which are less than seven years, we have 2520 days, which are prophetically equal to the same number of solar years. The end of these is the terminus of the times of the Babylonish kingdom of men, or of the Stump of the Babylonian Tree banded with iron and brass; that is, under its Latino-Greek constitution.

Judah and his companions have also *seven times* allotted to them, before they can obtain deliverance from Babylonish oppression and reproach. This appears from the twenty-sixth chapter of Leviticus and the eighteenth verse, which I render as follows:—" If ye will not yet for all this hearken unto me, then *I will increase to punish you seven times for your sins.*" This threat is repeated four several times in the same chapter. It cannot mean four distinct punishments of seven years each, or seven punishments. The history of the nation forbids this interpretation: it can therefore only signify that, if they would persist in their transgressions of the law, notwithstanding all the chastisements they experienced while living in Jehovah's sight upon his land, he would bring upon them a punishment of *seven prophetic times' duration*, or 2520 years.

But at what national epoch should this 2520 years of adversity commence? They cannot begin with any event connected with the Ten Tribes of Israel; because the latest, which is their expulsion from the Holy Land, B. C. 724 and 9 months, would cause them to have terminated A. D. 1795 and 3 months, since which time we still find them groaning under the oppression and reproach of the Babylonish Powers and their populations. Our inquiry, then, is limited to the history of Judah subsequently to the expulsion of the Ten Tribes. After this calamity the remnant of these tribes mingled themselves with Judah; and in their history we find nothing of any note as an epoch but the celebrated Passover in the eighteenth of Josiah's reign. Of this it is written, "There was no passover like to that kept in Israel from the days of Samuel the prophet." It was a royal effort to bring the nation to repentance, that the threatened chastisement of the Law might be averted. "Notwithstanding, the Lord turned not from the fierceness of his great wrath, wherewith his anger was kindled against Judah. . . . And he said, I will remove Judah also out of my sight, as I have removed Israel, and will cast off this city Jerusalem which I have chosen, and the temple of which I said, My name shall be there." In seventeen years after this, that is, in the first of Nebuchadnezzar's reign, the dominion of Babylon overshadowed the kingdom of Judah. The seven times had become current. Still in judgment the God of Israel remembers mercy; for he says, "If they shall confess their iniquity . . . and their uncircumcised hearts be humbled: . . . Then will I remember my covenant with Jacob; and also my covenants with Isaac and with Abraham will I remember; and *I will remember the land*. . . . And yet for all that they have done, when they be in the land of their enemies, *I will not cast them away*, neither will I abhor them to destroy them utterly, and to break my covenant with them; for I am Jehovah their God."

But the probability of Josiah's passover being an epoch in Judah's Calendar is converted into certainty by Ezekiel. He says, "Now it came to pass *in the thirtieth year* I was among the captives by the river of Chebar, which was the fifth year of king Jehoiachin's captivity."[1] In another place, he says, "It came to pass *in the seven and twentieth year* the word of the Lord came unto me."[2] After identifying the thirtieth year with the fifth of Jehoiachin's captivity, he dates the communications he receives from the Lord by the year of the captivity until the seven and twentieth, which was the sixteenth year after Jerusalem was smitten.[3] This seems to have been the latest, which was therefore the *fifty-second year* from the passover. But why did he not continue to date *from the passover* instead of from *the captivity?* The reason was evidently because, as the captivity was for 70 years, he preferred to mark its diminution for the encouragement of his brethren, than to note the lapse of time from the passover, which being the epoch of a long series of ages, was calculated to depress the national mind by reminding it of the remoteness of its deliverance.

The thirtieth year period is thus accounted for. Josiah reigned thirty-one years; and the passover being in the eighteenth year of his reign, a remainder is left of *thirteen* years. Jehoahaz his son reigned *three months*. He was succeeded by his brother Jehoiakim, who reigned *eleven* years. Next was Jehoiachin, who reigned *three months and three days*, and was then carried off to Babylon, and Zedekiah set

(1) Ezek. i. 1, 2.   (2) Ezek. xxix. 17.   (3) Ezek. xxxiii. 21.

up in his place. Here were 29 years, 6 months, and 10 days, inclusive of the fifth of Jehoiakim's captivity, or the *thirtieth* from the passover, as Ezekiel states; that is, B. C. 626 and 9 months. Seeing, then, that he has made it a point of departure for a calculation of years, I think that we cannot do better than to coincide with him, and to add on to these the remainder of Judah's 2520.

Another epoch, however, must be sought for the commencement of Babylon's 2520 years. These are Babylon's seven times in its relation to Judah; and must therefore be calculated from the epoch of Judah's first subjection to its dominion. This happened in the 4th of Jehoiakim's reign, which was also the first of Nebuchadnezzar's, and B. C. 608. In this year Jeremiah prophesied that Judah and the surrounding nations should be subject to the King of Babylon for 70 years; and that at the end of these, in the reign of his grandson, many nations and great kings should serve themselves of him;[1] that is, make the Babylonish kingdom their own: all of which has come to pass to the very letter.

There seems to be a remarkable fitness in commencing the seven times of the kingdom of Babylon with the beginning of Nebuchadnezzar's reign; inasmuch as he may be regarded as the second, or modern, founder of the state, Nimrod being the first. "Is not this great Babylon," said he, "that I have built for the capital of the kingdom by the might of my power, and for the honor of my majesty? While the word was in the king's mouth, there fell a voice from heaven saying, O king Nebuchadnezzar, to thee it is spoken; The kingdom is departed from thee! And seven times shall pass over thee, until thou know that the Most High hath power over the kingdom of men, and giveth it to whomsoever he will."

Admitting, then, these epochs for a beginning, Judah's seven times will terminate in the common A. D. 1893 and 3 months; and Babylon's, A. D. 1911. Judah's period is thus spoken of by Hosea: "I will be unto Ephraim, saith Jehovah, as a lion, and as a young lion to the house of Judah: I, even I, will tear and go away; I will take away and none shall rescue. I will go and return to my place, *till they acknowledge their offence*, and seek my face: in their affliction they will seek me early." This is their seven-times condition. The particular "affliction," called in Jeremiah "the time of Jacob's trouble,"[2] has not yet come upon them. "Alas!" he exclaims, in the prospect of it, "for that day is great, so that none is like it: it is even the time of Jacob's trouble; but he shall be saved out of it. For it shall come to pass in that day, saith Jehovah of armies, that I will break his (the Russo-Gogian Autocrat's) yoke from off thy neck, and will burst thy bonds; and *strangers shall* NO MORE *serve themselves of Jacob*: but they shall serve Jehovah their God, and the Beloved their King, whom I will *raise up* unto them" from the dead.[3] This is the "time of trouble" spoken of by Daniel, and yet future. Now, in view of this, Hosea represents them as saying to one another, "Come, and let us return unto Jehovah: for he hath torn, and he will heal us: he hath smitten, and he will bind us up. *After two days* he will revive us: *in the third day* he will raise us up, and we shall live in his sight."[4] These days are three periods of a thousand years each. The *two days* are past, and the nation is now *in the third day* of its smitten condition, 2479 years of the seven times having passed away. The posterity of Jacob have advanced 479 years into "the third day." Thus it is, that as the Beloved, or אֵת דָּוִד *aith dāwid*, their king, was raised up bodily in the third day; so, after the similitude thereof shall his nation be politically (and many of them as literally as he) raised up to live in Jehovah's sight,[5] that is, in their fatherland, in the current day of the seven times.

Woe be to the kingdom of Babylon when the political resurrection of Israel occurs;[6] for "*much torment and sorrow*" are decreed against its populations during the last forty years of its existence. This will appear from the testimony of Micah.

---

(1) Jer. xxvi. 1–11; xxvii. 7. (2) Jer. xxx. 7. (3) Acts ii. 30.
(4) Hos. vi. 1, 2. (5) 2 Kings xvii. 23. (6) Ezek. xxxvii. 1–14.

The prophet in behalf of his countrymen supplicates Jehovah, saying, "Feed thy people with thy rod, the flock of thine heritage, which dwell solitarily in the wood (alone and not reckoned of the nations) in the midst of Carmel, let them feed in Bashan and Gilead, *in the days of old*." To this Jehovah replies, "*According to the days of thy coming out of the land of Egypt* will I show unto him (Israel) marvellous things. *The nations shall see* and be confounded at all their might: they shall lay their hand upon their mouth, their ears shall be deaf. *They shall lick the dust like a serpent*, they shall move out of their strongholds as creeping things of the earth: they shall be afraid of the Lord our God, and shall fear because of thee," O Israel. There can be no mistake here. History proves that since the prophet wrote this it has never come to pass. It is therefore in the future. Israel were forty years passing from Egypt to Canaan; they will consequently be forty years in passing from their enemies' lands of the Babylonian dominion into the Holy Land to dwell there as an independent nation. In this their transit through "the wilderness of the people"[1] they will have to fight their way; and in so doing make the Babylonian nations "lick the dust like a serpent;" a phrase very appropriate to the prostration of the Serpent power.

Here, then, are 40 years to be deducted from the seven times of Babylon for the period during which the Holy Ones and their people are "taking away its dominion to consume and to destroy it unto the end."[2] This brings us back from the common A. D. 1911 to A. D. 1872. But before Israel and the Holy Ones can enter upon this work, Michael, the great commander, must stand up, and the Holy ones must be raised from the dead; and a communication must be established between Israel and the land of their enemies and their future commanders: for the reason given for their fighting against the sons of Greece is "because the Lord is with them, and shall be seen over them." The Lord, then, will have come as the Ancient of Days at some time previous to 1872: how is that epoch to be approached?

In reply to this inquiry it may be remarked, that nothing can be done by Israel without the Saints or Holy Ones; therefore it must be ascertained what is testified of them, that it may be seen, if possible, when they appear upon the arena of debate.

The seventh of Daniel reveals that the Holy Ones sojourning under the dominion of the Latino-Babylonian power, or Papacy, that is, Papal Europe, are to be given over to its power to the end of a time, times, and the dividing of time, or 1260 years. This period is manifestly not completed. Their oppressor and destroyer still exists in full force, as far as they are concerned; and will continue so till their resurrection. Now the element of the power that has moved heaven and earth for their destruction is that represented by *the Eyes and Mouth* of the Little Three-horn subduer. The Eyes and Mouth power is evidently the chief actor against the holy ones, the horn in which they are placed being subordinate to its will. The 1260 years of its prevalence against them must therefore be calculated from the institution of the Eyes and Mouth as a power of the Babylonian dominion; which institution would be equivalent to "The King honoring a god of guardians in his estate or realm; and acknowledging and increasing him with glory;"[3] and not from the first appearance of the Ten Horns, or of the Little One that came up after them and subdued three of them. Now, the acknowledgment of the Eyes and Mouth as *the god of the Kingdom of Babylon*, or "god upon earth," as the pope is styled, was in the reign of Phocas; who wrote to the Latin Bishop in the common A. D. 604, and acknowledged his supremacy over all other ecclesiastics of the realm. This private recognition was followed by an imperial decree in the common A. D. 606, and in two years after, as before

---

(1) Ezek. xx. 35.   (2) Dan. vii. 11, 26.   (3) Dan. xi. 38, 39.

mentioned, a pillar was erected commemorative of the event, with the date of A. D. 608, inscribed upon it. This may have been only the date of the erection of the pillar. If the common era were the true one, it would be a remarkable coincidence, that the *secular* Babylonish power under Nebuchadnezzar commenced its career of prevailing against Judah, the saints' people, B. C. 608 and 9 months; and that a pillar bearing the same date after Christ should memorialize the institution of the *Spiritual* Babylonish power under the "strange god," who should signalize his career by making war against the saints themselves, and in prevailing against them. But the coincidence vanishes when we come to understand that the common A. D. 606 is 609 years from the birth of Christ. The coincidence, therefore, is really between the first of Nebuchadnezzar and the common A. D. 606. Is it not safe then to select for the beginning of the period which is to end at the coming of the Ancient of Days, the common A. D. 606? The analogy pointed out would favor it; the date of the Phocian decree confirm it. My conviction is that the judgment upon Babylon will be *announced* as about to sit; and that the Ancient of Days and the saints will meet "in the air" and among the clouds,[1] in the common A. D. 1866, or 1260 years from A. D. 606.

At the end of this period, then, the saints are delivered. The papacy, with all the power it can stir up, cannot make successful war upon them any more; we must not, however, conclude from this that the Latino-Babylonian confederacy will be immediately dissolved, and powerless. It has power to make war after the resurrection, though not successfully; for it is written of it, "Power was given to him (the Beast representing the confederacy) ποιησαι, poiësai, to practise *forty and two months*," or 1260 years. These must therefore end at the termination of the seven times of Babylon's existence; and constitute the period indicated in Dan. xii. 7, which is marked by the concentration of the power of the Twelve Tribes.

Taking the resurrection, then, at A. D. 1866, there will be an interval between that event and the beginning of Micah's forty years A. D. 1872, of six years. Is the Russo-Gogian Autocracy broken by the Stone-power before or after the end of this six-year period? I should answer, *Before it.* Again; Is it broken to pieces before or after the resurrection of the saints? It is most likely *after it*; for speaking of the destruction of the Clay Power; that is, of a power that "ladeth itself with thick clay," by gathering unto it all nations, and heaping unto it all people, and thus accumulating what does not belong to it; Habbakuk says to its chief, "Shall they not *rise up* פתע, pĕthă, in the twinkling of an eye that shall bite thee, and *awake* that shall vex thee? . . . For *the Stone* shall cry out of the wall, and *the beam* out of the timber shall answer it. . . . For the earth shall be filled with the knowledge of the glory of Jehovah, as the waters cover the sea. . . . Jehovah is in his holy palace; be silent all the earth before him." This is evidently a prediction of the resurrection of the power that is to destroy the Clay-dominion. The Clay-power stands unconsciously waiting for this in the Holy Land and City. The saints gathered unto Christ in the air will be witnesses of its prostration as Israel were of Pharaoh's, without drawing a sword. All the glory of this will be due to the Ancient of Days, with whom none coöperate in the infliction of the first disaster upon the enemy, which is by pestilence, mutual slaughter, hail, and thunder-bolts, from heaven. This cripples, but does not finally destroy the dominion. It is as a Moscow to Napoleon, which required repeated blows for the destruction of his power. Christ and the holy ones descend from the clouds for the purpose of grinding the shattered fragments of the Russo-Gogian Image to powder. The Lion-man, the Bear, and the Leopard, or the gold, the silver, and the brass, must have their dominion taken away. These are borderers upon the Holy Land, and will demand the immediate attention of the Stone and Beam out of the tim-

---

(1) 1 Thess. iv. 17.

ber; "who shall waste the land of Assyria with the sword, and the land of Nimrod in the entrances thereof: thus shall Israel be delivered from the Assyrian, when he cometh into the land, and when he treadeth within their borders."[1] It would seem that the taking of the saints up into the air will be to separate them from those who are to be the objects of divine indignation; and to place them above the falling artillery of the clouds. For these reasons and others that might be adduced, it may be concluded that the resurrection will precede the overthrow of the Russian hosts upon the mountains of Israel.

But the holy ones raised from the dead, and Jerusalem and the Holy Land delivered, by A. D. 1866, which is also the ending of the 1335 years, "the Lord Jehovah (in Greek *Jesus*) is in his holy palace," and for a time " all the earth is silent before him," and trembling in expectation of judgment. At this crisis, He is as " an Ensign upon the mountains;" and the tranquillity of the epoch is " as dry heat impending lightning, as a cloud of dew in the sultriness of harvest." It will then be said of Jerusalem, *"The Lord is there."* The remnant of Judah in the land for *the seven months ensuing* the fall of Gog on the mountains of Israel will be occupied in burying the dead, and cleansing its surface of the slain.[2] The destruction of Pharaoh and his host, which, with the plagues of Egypt, were well known to all that generation, did not cause the nations to confederate and to rush upon Moses and his people to swallow them up; nor did it forty years after deter the seven nations of Canaan from combining to preserve their country from conquest by Israel. It is true that when, in addition to this, they heard that the Lord dried up the waters of Jordan, and that the two Amorite powers east of that river had been exterminated, "their hearts melted, neither was their spirit in them any more;" nevertheless, the kings assembled their armies and contended for five years in numerous battles against Israel. Though melted with fear, they found no chance of escape but in resistance. Extermination was decreed against them. Death without resistance or with it was their only alternative; they accepted the latter, and perished sword in hand by the armies of Israel.

After the same type will it be with the seven strong Latin Kingdoms of the Babylonian dominion after the fall of the Czar and his hosts, the Pharaoh of modern times. Micah says, "Their ears shall be deaf." Whatever news may greet them from the Holy Land, will have no more effect upon the powers than Jehovah's message to Pharaoh. They are to be dashed in pieces as a potter's vessel; submission or resistance, the result will be the same. Fair warning, however, will be given, that Israel and their friends who, believing in the bursting forth of impending vengeance, may desire to escape it, may separate themselves from those who determine to resist. "I will be still, saith the Lord; yet in my dwelling-place I will be without fear." This is subsequently to A. D. 1866—*an awful pause* between the treading of the Edom and Jehoshaphat winepress, and the Lord's roaring out of Zion, and uttering his voice from Jerusalem.[3]

In the silence of this truce of God, what is the great movement of the time? The question may be answered in the words of Isaiah, that the Lord having beaten off the enemy from the channel of the river (Euphrates) to the stream of Egypt, (the Nile,) it shall come to pass that *the great trumpet shall then be blown,* and the Israelites shall come who were ready to perish in the land of Assyria, and the outcasts in the land of Egypt, and shall worship the Lord in the holy mount at Jerusalem.[4] Another prophet says, "The Lord God shall blow the trumpet," when he shall be seen over Israel.[5] This is the period referred to in the " memorial of blowing of trumpets" on the first day of the seventh month under the Law.[6] Two trumpets will be blown. By the blowing of the first the princes, heads of

(1) Mic. v. 6.   (2) Ezek. xxxix. 11–16.   (3) Joel iii. 16.
(4) Isai. xxvii. 12; xvii. 3.   (5) Zech. ix. 14.   (6) Lev. xxiii. 24.

the thousands of Israel, called the holy ones, are gathered unto the Lord; and when the second is also blown, all Israel's hosts will begin to assemble towards the dwelling-place of their King.[1]

The trumpet to be blown by the Anointed One of Jehovah, styled the Lord God, is *a proclamation to the world*, to which it is announced by some of the remaining third part of Judah which escapes the calamities attendant upon the invasion of their land by the Russo-Gogian armies, and their overthrow. As it is written, "I will send מהם, *maihem*, of those that escape to the nations, to Tarshish, Pul, and Lud, משכי קשת, *mōshkai kĕshĕth*, sounders of truth;* to Tubal and Javan, the coasts far off that have not heard my fame, neither have seen my glory; and they shall declare my glory among the nations."[2] "The Lord gives the word; great is the company of those that publish it."[3]

This company is apocalyptically represented as an "angel flying in the midst of the (Babylonian) heaven;" and the truth they sound out about the fame and glory of the Lord is styled "a good message of the age," ευαγγελιον αιωνιον, *euaggelion aiōnion*, pertaining to the age. It commands the nations to transfer their allegiance to God, under penalty of the judgment in case of refusal. Its words are, "Fear God, and give glory to him: *for the hour of his judgment is come;*" and to Israel scattered in all the Kingdom of Babylon, and in its capital especially, the proclamation saith, "Come out of her, my people, that ye be not partakers of her sins, and that ye receive not of her plagues."[4]

The sounding of this proclamation will cause a general movement among the Jews, who will be allured by it, and prepare to leave the lands of their captivity. "I will *allure* her, saith the Lord, and bring her into the wilderness, and speak friendly to her heart."[5] As to the Latino-Babylonian powers of Europe, they will be stirred up to war by the proclamation. In the Apocalypse they are styled, the Beast, the

---

(1) Numb. x. 1–7. (2) Isai. lxvi. 19. (3) Psal. lxviii. 11.
(4) Rev. xiv. 6, 7; xviii. 4. (5) Hos. ii. 14; Ezek. xx. 35.

---

* Translators of Isaiah have been considerably at a loss what to do with *mōshkai kĕshĕth*. The first word some have thought should be rendered *Meshech*, called *Moschi* by the Greeks, as a proper name; seeing it is associated with Tubal as in other places. Boothroyd has so rendered it, and Lowth is inclined to it, as appears from his notes; but in the text he renders the phrase "*who draw the bow,*" in common with the English Version. But though it cannot be denied that the words may be literally rendered thus, this rendering certainly does not apply in this place. "*Who draw the bow*" is not at all more characteristic of Tarshish, Pul, and Lud, than of Tubal and Javan, of whom it is not affirmed. They all drew the bow in battle when the prophet wrote; and Tarshish at the present time is more famous for gunpowder and cannon-balls than for bows and arrows.

The literal sense of the words cannot, therefore, be the proper one in this place. I have rendered it "*sounders of truth,*" which is in agreement with what is affirmed of those sent, saying, "And they shall *declare my glory* (or sound the truth) among the nations."

Moshkai comes from *māshăkh*, to draw: *māshăkh haz-zĕra* signifies literally *to draw the seed*, or figuratively *to sow;* because the seed is *drawn* out from the bag to be scattered. Also the phrase *māshăkh hy-yōvail*, literally *to draw the trumpet*. This expresses the real action in sounding a trumpet before the blast is given; hence the figurative word for *māshăkh* here is *to sound;* that is, it signifies "to sound" *by implication*.

The word *kĕshĕth* literally signifies *a bow:* but *the bending of the tongue in speech* is likened to a bow in Scripture, as, "they bend their tongue like a bow for lies." It may also be bent like a bow for truth. In process of time the last letter of the word called *Thav* was regarded as a radical, and changed into another called *Teth*, being written without the points, *k-sh-t* instead of *k-sh-th:* hence the Chaldee *kushtā* for the Hebrew *kāshthā*, pronounced *kāshtā*, "to shoot with a bow."

The words *kĕshĕth* and *kŏshet*, then, may be taken as the same. By turning to Gesenius under the last word it will be found to signify both *a bow*, and *truth*. Hence, *mōshkai kĕshĕth* are drawers of truth. They are sent *to draw the great trumpet of the Lord God, the sound* of which is the declaration of his glory among the nations that had not previously heard of his fame nor seen his glory. Drawers of truth, then, are sounders or proclaimers of truth, apocalyptically styled, *euangelion aiōnion*, "the good message pertaining to the age."

False Prophet, and the Kings of the earth; of whom it is said, "they and their armies, gathered together to make war against the Lamb, and against his army."[1] When this war actually breaks out, the contest will be between the Jews as the Lord's army, and the armies of the Babylonian kings; and is styled, "the war of the Great-day of God Almighty." The period of its continuance is the day during which "the judgment sits upon Daniel's fourth beast;" and the result of which is, the "thrones are cast down," and their kingdoms become Jehovah's and his Christ's. When this is consummated the seven times of the Kingdom of Men will be fully exhausted. The time allotted to the blowing of the great trumpet will be, I doubt not, several years. There will be much to accomplish among the nations which do not belong to the Latino-Greek Babylonian dominion. Jehovah did not send Israel against the Canaanites till forty years after the fall of Pharaoh; and although it will not be so long as this, I have reason to believe, that the war between the Jews and the Papal Powers will not begin until several years after the smiting of the Russo-Gogian Image, or at least till A. D. 1882.

The great trumpet to be blown announces that "the *hour* of God's judgment is come;" and in the apostrophe upon the fate of Babylon it is said, "in *one hour* is thy judgment come." Now, in that judgment, not only Rome, but the Papacy, or False Prophet-power, the imperial Beast that sustains it, and the Papal Governments and nations are judged. The time therefore in judging, or executing vengeance upon the one, is the period of judgment for them all. At that crisis they will all be confederates in arms against Christ and his armies; for it is written concerning the papal powers, represented by the Ten Horns, or Ten Toes of the Russo-Gogian Image, "they shall receive power as kings *one hour* with the Beast," or Little Horn with the Eyes and Mouth. "These have one mind, and shall give their power and strength to the beast." "For God hath put in their hearts to fulfil his will, and to agree, and give their kingdom to the beast, until the words of God shall be fulfilled." "These shall make war with the Lamb." Therefore, John says, "I saw the beast and the kings of the earth, and their armies gathered together to make war against him and against his army." "But the Lamb shall overcome them:" for "the beast was taken, and with him the false prophet, and cast alive into the lake of fire; and the remnant were slain with the sword of the King of kings and Lord of lords,"[2] that is, *by Israel*, as shown elsewhere.

Now the use of the words *hour* and *one hour*, in these places, is not without precise signification. They are not used vaguely or indefinitely. They are figurative of an exact number of solar years, which number is *the twelfth of a time*. Bible days are twelve hours long; so that an hour is the twelfth part of a daytime. If the time be an ενιαυτος, *eniautos*, that which returns upon itself, with another twelfth termed a *month*, then an hour signifies only *thirty days*, being diminished by the greater term, as in Rev. ix. 15; but if it stand absolutely, that is, with no other sign to qualify it, it signifies *thirty years*, or the twelfth of a time of 360 years. While touching upon this point, I may remark that *half an hour* is used apocalyptically as significative of years in the saying, "there was silence in the heaven about the space of half an hour;" that is, between the opening of the Seventh Seal and the casting fire upon the earth—*a period of fourteen years*, being "about the space," but not quite "*half an hour*," which is *fifteen years*. The meaning of the saying is, "*There was peace among the rulers for fourteen years*," or from A. D. 323 to 337, as may be seen by reference to Gibbon's Decline and Fall of the Roman Empire.

Thirty years, then, being the duration of an hour in these places, the confederacy of the papal powers will continue thirty years, during which judgment is being

---

(1) Rev. xix. 19; xvii. 14.   (2) Rev. xvii. and xix.

executed upon them by the people of the holy ones, who torment them with all the calamities of war. This thirty years' war is the grinding of the shattered elements of the Image to powder by the Stone, and ending with the annihilation of Babylon at the expiration of its 2520 years, necessarily begins A. D. 1882.

But besides the 2300 years, the seventy heptades of 490 years, and the two periods of 1260 years each, there are other two periods that yet remain to be explained. These are one of 1290 years, and another of 1335 years. The former period relates to the desolation of the Holy Land and its desolator; the latter, to the resurrection of the Holy Ones, of whom the prophet had the assurance of being one.

The 1290 years are noted in the eleventh verse of the twelfth chapter; which, however, as it stands in the English version, cannot possibly be understood. From this the reader would suppose that the 1290 years should be calculated from the taking away of the daily; that is, from the suppression of sacrifice when the Roman power destroyed Jerusalem, A. D. 72: but in that case, "*that determined*" should then have began to be poured out upon the desolator, which every one knows was not the fact.

The proper rendering of this text is, "*And after the time the daily shall be removed, even for to set up an abomination making desolate a thousand two hundred and ninety days.*" The time referred to in this place, is the Seventy Heptades of 490 years; "after" the lapse of this time, "the evening-morning sacrifice," or תמיד, *tāmīd*, should be removed. But, how long would it be after the end of this time ere the daily should be removed? The answer to this question was one of the times and seasons which the Father had put in his own power;[1] therefore, Jesus said, "Of that day and hour knoweth no man, no, not the angels which are in heaven, *neither the Son*, but the Father. Take ye heed, watch and pray: for *ye know not when the time is.*"[2] This he said to his apostles; but since then "the day and hour" have passed away; and we know that Judah's tribulation, characterized by the removal of the daily, the casting down of the foundation of its sanctuary and the law, and the destruction of their commonwealth, occurred A. D. 72.

Now, the daily was removed for "the overspreading of abominations until the consummation, and that determined should be poured upon the desolator."[3] One of these abominations was to prevail for upwards of twelve hundred years, and to be found in desolating possession of the land at the end of 1290. As every one knows, this desolator of the Holy Land thus far is the Ottoman Power, a "time-of-the-end" representative of the long-prevailing "abomination." The 1290 were to end when the time came to pour out upon the desolator; it is evident, therefore, they could not begin A. D. 72. The text does not require that they should; and the passage last quoted shows that they were to end *at the period of pouring out* upon the desolator; that is, when the 1290 years should end, the pouring out of that determined upon the Ottoman should begin. It is well known that there has been a notable pouring out of calamities upon this power from A. D. 1820 to the present time. But the end is not immediately; for the pouring out period is *to* continue "*until the consummation,*" which is marked by the initiation of the restitution of Israel's power. If the Ottoman were demolished in a month, there would still be an outpouring in reserve for the desolator in actual occupation of Jerusalem at the advent of the Ancient of Days. This will be the power constituted of the Greeks and Latins under the Autocrat of all the Russias, as before explained. His will be the last *régime* of the desolating abomination; and when the judgments of the Sixth Vial, which dry up the Euphratean Power,[4] are exhausted, the desolation of Jerusalem and the Holy Land will terminate in the helpless annihilation of their Gentile destroyers, both Muscovite and Turk.

(1) Acts i. 7.   (2) Mark xiii. 32.   (3) Dan. ix. 27.   (4) Rev. xvi. 12.

Lastly, 45 years after the end of the 1290 years, the period of the Little Horn of the West's prevalence over the Holy Ones is brought to a close. This period, it will be remembered, is 1260 years long. The *end of it* is designated by that of the 1335 years, which have a beginning in common with the 1290. They commence 75 years before the 1260, being times pertaining to the Heirs of the Holy Land, or Kings of the East; and therefore part of Judah's times; while the 1260 are a part of the times of the kingdom of Babylon—the period of its prevalence against the Holy Ones and their people; and consequently to be calculated from a different beginning, though ending at the same epocha—A. D. 1865–6. "*Blessed he that expects and* יגיע, *yághia,* LABORS *for the thousand three hundred and five and thirty days.*" This is the text in which the 1335 years are noted; and the only place in the Bible where they are to be found. To look and labor for them is to watch for the end of them, and to strive to attain what is to be manifested at their expiration. When they terminate, the resurrection of the dead predicted in Dan. xii. 2, will come to pass; for the revelator said to the prophet, " Be thou to thyself אתה לך, *áthiah laik,* till the end: for thou shalt rest, and תעמד, *thiámōd,** arise to thine inheritance at the end of the days." The days last mentioned in the context are the 1335, and must therefore be the days referred to. Daniel was to be to himself till the end of these days, till which time he was to be at rest, "sleeping in the dust of the earth." This is his present condition, mere dust and ashes of the tomb recently discovered in Persia. But in a few years, that is, about 1866, when the 1335 years terminate, he will " arise to his inheritance" in the kingdom of God.

In conclusion, let the reader observe, that it is not merely he that desires or looks for the end of the 1335 days who is pronounced "blessed." There are many who desire the resurrection of the wise, and, as Balaam, would like to be of the number; but who either give themselves no trouble to attend to it, or are ignorant of the means of attainment, or will only labor for it according to their own suppositions of possibilities. These suppose every thing, but prove nothing. The blessedness of the resurrection is a laborious acquisition—a contention for the mastery over ourselves, and the world around us. This can only be attained by the " taught of God," who understand his doctrine, and yield it the faithful and self-sacrificing obedience he requires. Then "labor to enter into his rest;" " for many shall seek to enter in and shall not be able." They will be excluded from the Kingdom of God because they have not sought entrance into it in the appointed way. " Seek first the Kingdom of God," saith the Great Teacher, " and his righteousness." How highly important is this exhortation now, seeing that in about a dozen years the resurrection will have transpired, and no further invitation to inherit it presented to the world. Ought we not then to awake to earnestness, and by a rigid scrutiny of our faith and practice, obtain a scriptural satisfaction, if we shall be able to stand unabashed before the Judge of the living and the dead? The glory that shall follow is great for the approved. The world is theirs,[1] when all nations come and do homage before the Prince of Israel, because his judgments are made manifest.[2] But before they can have "power over the nations,"[3] they must bind the strong that rule them. This is their mission at the end of the 1335 years: " To execute vengeance upon the nations, and punishment upon the peoples; to bind their kings with chains, and their nobles with fetters of iron; to execute upon them the judgment written: this honor have all his saints." From A. D. 1866 to A. D. 1911, a period of over forty years, they will be engaged in this work, and in the organizing the world upon new and better principles. When this work is finished we shall have what is styled "*the world to come.*" The king-

---

* It is used in this sense in Lev. xix. 16, where it is rendered *rise up.*

(1) 1 Cor. iii. 21, 22.   (2) Rev. xv. 4.   (3) Rev. ii. 26.

doms, empires, and republics now existing, will be but shadows of the past eclipsing righteousness and truth—blots upon the page of human story. The Kingdom of Babylon among the rest will have passed through all its phases of iniquity and crime, and at length have disappeared like chaff before the wind, being ground to powder by the kingdom of God, which as a great mountain fills the whole earth.¹ The nations and their rulers will then heartily respond to the exhortation, saying, "Make a joyful noise to Jehovah, all the earth: make a loud noise, and rejoice and sing praise. Sing unto Jehovah with the harp; with the harp, and the voice of a psalm. With trumpets and sound of cornets make a joyful noise before Jehovah, the King. Let the sea roar, and the fulness thereof; the world and they that dwell therein. Let the floods clap their hands; let the hills be joyful together before Jehovah; for he cometh to rule the earth; with righteousness shall he rule the world, and with equity the peoples."²

Such is the solution of the Great Eastern question which has been providentially formed for the development of the terrible situation of A. D. 1868.

(1) Dan. ii. 35. (2) Ps. xcviii. 4–9.

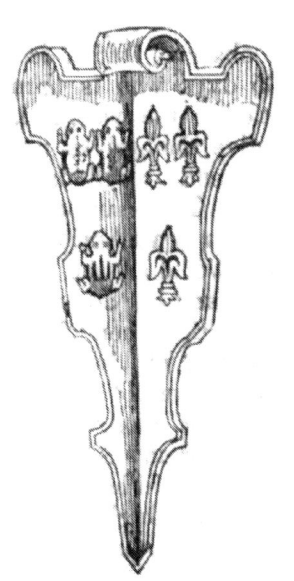

Armorial Shield of Clovis, the first Papal King of France.

CALENDAR

OF THE

SEVEN TIMES OF BABYLON AND JUDAH.

Anno Mundi.	Before Christ.	
3460	626	Nine months before this date the celebrated passover from which Ezekiel dates his thirtieth year was held in the 18th of Josiah, king of Judah's reign. Henceforth Jehovah punishes Israel *seven times*, or 2520 years, for their sins.
3478	608	The 4th of Jehoiakim, and 1st of Nebuchadnezzar's reign. The subjection of the nations to his *régime* for 70 years begins. Also the Seven Times of the kingdom of Babylon, during the greater part of which it is the Tree-Stump banded with Iron and Brass.
3479	607	A representation is made to Nebuchadnezzar in a dream of the destruction of the Babylonian dominion by the Kingdom of God in the Latter Days.
3529	557	The 1st of Belshatzar's reign. It is shown to Daniel that the power of the Kingdom of God for the consumption and destruction of the Babylonish empire will be manifested through the Son of Man, the Holy Ones, and their people, at the end of 1260 years.
3532	554	The 3d of Belshatzar. It is revealed to Daniel that sacrifice should be abolished, the temple again destroyed, the law suppressed, and Judah and the Holy Land trodden under foot 2300 years by the fourth Babylonian régime more especially; and which should be afterwards overthrown by Judah's Commander-in-Chief.
3548	538	The end of Nebuchadnezzar's dynasty. The 1st of Darius the Mede. It is revealed to Daniel what should come to pass in relation to the Son of Man during the last seven years of the first 490 years of the 2300 evening-morning: and before the abolition of Mosaic sacrifice, the precise time of which, called "*the day and hour*," is not revealed.
3551	535	The 3d year of Cyrus, or first of his sole reign. The characteristic features of the 2300 years that remain over from the fall of the Persian administration are revealed to the prophet. Also the central points of the Eastern Question radiating into the expulsion of the Gentiles from the Holy Land, the deliverance of Judah, and the restoration of Israel's power, after the 2300 years are ended. Cyrus makes proclamation for the rebuilding of the temple. Daniel dies.
3571	515	The 2d of Darius the Persian. He issues a decree enforcing that of Cyrus. Seventy years from the burning of the temple in the 19th of Nebuchadnezzar's reign.
3575	511	The sixth of Darius, being 70 years from the 23d of Nebuchadnezzar, when 745 persons were carried captive to Babylon. The building of the temple finished.
3619	467	The 7th of Artaxerxes, who issues a decree this year for the restoration of the Commonwealth of Judah.

Anno Mundi	Before Christ	
3632	454	The 20th of Artaxerxes. Issues a second decree authorizing the building of the waste places and the walls of Jerusalem. *Commencement of the Seventy Heptades, and of the 2300 years.*
3755	331	Darius Codomannus slain. End of the Silver Régime of the Babylonian Image, the Bear and the Ram dynasties, 206 years and 9 months from the fall of Belshatzar. Alexander the Great reigns. The Tree-Stump banded with Brass.
3743	323	Alexander dies. The notable horn of the Goat, the kingdom of Grecia's first and mighty king, broken while he stands up, or without defeat.
3775	311	"Four kingdoms stand up out of the Goat-nation," represented by its four horns, and by the Four Heads of the Leopard. This is styled in Maccabees, "*The Era of the Greeks.*"
3919	167	Two years before the death of Antiochus Epiphanes. The Era of the Asmoneans.
3926	160	Judas Maccabeus dies. End of Ezekiel's 430 years, being the length of time from the burning of the temple by the Chaldeans.
4021	65	The empire of the Seleucidæ, or Kings of the North, annexed to Rome. The Tree-Stump banded with Iron. An observer in Judea at this crisis sees the Little Horn coming up out of the Northern Horn of the Goat, and waxing great against the east.
4049	37	Antigonus, the last of the Asmonean kings of Judea, put to death ignominiously by the Romans at the instance of Herod, whom they had set up as King of the Jews. The Little Horn waxes great against the glory of the land.
4056	30	Egypt, the Kingdom of the South, annexed to the Roman empire. The Little Horn is now "exceeding great," and stands upon the Babylonian earth the unrivalled "King that does according to his will."
4086	0	ANNUS DOMINI. The Prince Royal of Judah is born in Bethlehem six months after John the Baptist, Herod the Idumean having reigned thirty-seven years.
4089	8	Nine months after this date Herod dies, having reigned 40 years. Archelaus succeeds him. *The Vulgar Era begins.*
4114	28	John the Baptist is 28 years and 9 months old. The *sixty-ninth* of the seventy heptades ends at this date. John proclaims the speedy appearing of the King of Israel, saying, ἤγγικε ἡ βασιλεια των ουρανων, ĕggikĕ hē basileia tōn ouranōn, *the royal dignity of the heavens has approached;* "I come immersing in water that he may be made manifest to Israel."
4116	30	Jesus being immersed of John, on coming up out of the Jordan is anointed from heaven with the Holy Spirit; and proclaimed by the Father before the assembled multitude as His Son, in whom he is well pleased. The Prince being thus manifested, the sceptre soon departs from Judah.
4117	31	Nine months after this date John is imprisoned. Henceforth Jesus preaches the Gospel of the Kingdom, assisted by his disciples.
4122	35	Pontius Pilate the Roman Governor of Judea. *The sceptre gone;* the Jews protesting that they had "*no other king than Cæsar.*" Three months after the commencement of this year we arrive at the month Nisan, on the 14th of which is the Passover. The 490 years of the Seventy Heptades end on this day. The Little Horn of the Goat magnifies itself against the Prince Royal at the instigation of the rulers of the Jews. He is tried, condemned, and crucified— וְאֵין לֹו wĕ-ain lo — *but nothing in him* is found; that is, he is without fault, as Pilate declared. Judah's rebellion is perfected by this condemnation of the innocent; by whose death sin-offerings are made complete;